The Heart

of

Ibiza

A true story of love, endurance and survival
against overwhelming odds.

Shirley Ann Lamens

First paperback edition December 2023

Book cover design by Design Office UK

Ibiza images courtesy of Ibiza Tourist Board of Consell d'Eivissa

Medical LVAD Image courtesy of Abbott

Paperback ISBN 978-1-7395106-0-2

eBook ISBN (978-1-7395106-1-9

Published by Amazon KDP

Contents

The Heart of Ibiza

The priceless gift of life.

To all the families who have been able to kindly agree to organ donation after the heartbreaking loss of a loved one.

The Heart of Ibiza

CHAPTER 1

A Very Close Call

"Why have you left it so long mate?" asked the paramedic as he shoved an aspirin the size of his palm in Richard's mouth and told him to chew on it.

It was about 12 o'clock in the afternoon and our youngest daughter Kate called me saying, "I don't think Daddy is very well." "When I asked if he was okay or if he wanted me to call you, his reply was, if you ring anybody you should call 999."

At this point I held my breath and asked Kate to stay with him. I called 999 from my work, which happened to be at our local hospital in Crewe. I went straight down to our A and E department (Accident and Emergency), to wait for my husband Richard to arrive. I also called Sue, my close friend, who lived just around the corner from us, to come and stay with Kate, who was only 14 at the time, until the paramedics arrived.

It felt like it was all happening in slow motion, but panic was slowly rising inside me. I waited in A and E with a friend and work colleague for what seemed like ages. Eventually I got a call from

Sue, to say that Richard wouldn't be coming to Leighton Hospital, but he was being taken to North Staffs Hospital. (Now called The Royal Stoke University Hospital).

I rushed home, my mind racing with all the thoughts of what may or may not be happening. I tried to get there before they went, but I was too late. Richard had already left with the ambulance on blue lights, 5 minutes before. The paramedics told our older daughter Jenny, who had now arrived at the house, not to try and follow the ambulance as they would be travelling at speed.

I asked the first responder paramedic if Richard was going to be alright and he wouldn't answer me, or look me in the eye. It was later I discovered why. I imagine that his ECG readings at the time, had been extremely alarming and there was great concern in his face.

CHAPTER 2

Shirley

So Much More than a Holiday Romance

It all began when my parents took me on my first holiday abroad in 1974, to Menorca, I was 14 years old. My dad decided it was the end of our holidays in the UK, with the previous few years being nothing but wet and dreary during the month of May. The rain always limited the activities you can do and sometimes it was cold every single day. They thought it was time to try somewhere warmer and the package holiday was becoming ever more popular and affordable. My brother and sister as both older than me, didn't holiday with us anymore so it was just the 3 of us.

My first school trip abroad to Switzerland, was the same year my parents had booked to go to Menorca. I couldn't believe it, after never having travelled outside of the UK, or been on a plane before. This is where my fascination with travel began, with the excitement and thrill of the airport experience, I felt this was an area I would like to work in when I was older.

On the beautiful island of Menorca, you arrive to see blue skies and feel the warm sunshine on your skin, the minute you step off the aircraft. The contrast to spending time on the mostly cold wet beaches of the UK wrapped in a towel or coat to keep you warm, was incredible.

We went on holiday to Menorca on a couple more occasions. Lorraine, my best friend from school, joined us with her parents as well as my sister Laura, who decided to tag along too. The Spanish waiters were like bees around a honey pot. Laura at 18, was given more freedom, but Lorraine and I were watched like hawks from the beady eyes of our parents.

My love of Ibiza began in 1976, when my parents booked a holiday there. They seemed to have truly got the travel bug and decided they wanted to try a different Spanish island and chose Ibiza. On reflection, I am so grateful they did, as my life seemed to be mapped out from the day I arrived. I was 17, it was my first year since leaving school and I had just started working as an invoice typist in Manchester.

Although Ibiza is known as the party island, there is something truly magical about it. The island's aura is difficult to explain, you probably feel it, or you don't. Once again this confirmed my enthusiasm for holidays and travel, I was well and truly hooked. That feeling again, as soon as those aircraft doors open, the warm air and sunshine embracing you, instantly putting you in the relaxed holiday mode. Ibiza has so many of the most beautiful sandy beaches and bays stretched over such a small island, it is most definitely worth a visit. At the time, I didn't realise how important this place would become for me and my future destiny.

We stayed in a small village called Cala Llonga, a quiet peaceful location on the East coast of the island. Cala Llonga has the most beautiful sweeping bay with clear waters, fringed with pine trees spreading down from the mountains and sheltering the bay. We stayed in a hotel called Playa Imperial, one of two hotels, set back above the bay, with beautiful views overlooking the sea.

A view of Cala Llonga bay

Image by VM – Vincent Mari

I first spotted Richard, as I was peering between the 2 hotels. From a large terrace you can look down to the pools and the long sandy beach and --- there he was. A tall, lean, and very tanned guy, with his tousled blonde curly hair, which looked a little scruffy. None the less he obviously drew my attention. I expected he was possibly Swedish or Danish, but certainly had the Scandinavian looks. I hadn't had a serious boyfriend at home yet, but if I was looking, I was always drawn to blond hair and blue eyes in appearance. Richard was mooring a speed boat and had just been water skiing. It seems strange when I think back, how he caught my eye in this way.

I discovered later who he was, when I saw him working as the DJ in the hotel we were staying in. I went up to ask him if he would play Barry White, as his taste in music wasn't really get up and dance and there was no one on the dance floor. His reply was flippant and a bit rude saying that he might – but he never did. Perhaps I appeared quite young in the eyes of Richard. I had only asked him to play a record, as I was on my own and feeling a little bored on holiday with my parents. That was the only contact and communication we had during that holiday, but how well I can remember that moment. It makes me laugh how he hasn't changed from that day, still sounding a bit sharp with his replies to things, but that's just the way he is and there is no malice in it whatsoever.

I would later find out, his personality was one of the strongest reasons that helped him on the road to recovery, when he was faced with the many health issues that happened later in our relationship.

The next year in 1977, my parents returned to Cala Llonga and asked if I wanted to come along, of course I did, this time taking another friend. We had gone to school together and always got on well. We were now a little older, so given a bit more freedom to go our own way, without the watchful eye of my parents.

I had forgotten all about Richard from the previous year and there was a different DJ working in the hotel. He organised entertainment evenings and events for the guests to take part in, this was a great way for my friend and I to spend our time.

One night, we decided to try another disco situated in the same village, some of the hotel staff had told us about this. To my surprise, when we arrived, there were very few people inside, but the one thing I noticed was the DJ, Richard. He had moved from the hotel and was now working for a local businessman who owned the disco, as well as other businesses in the area. Richard was still how I remembered him, tall, slim, with his slightly wild blonde hair and that same Scandinavian voice when he spoke.

I went up to him and said, "Hi do you remember me?" His reply was "Yes of course I do." He admitted later that he didn't remember me at all, but in his words, he thought I was a bit of all right and that was good enough for him.

From that point on, both our futures together were being made, even though we didn't know it at the time. I remember him coming up to me between playing records and we were able to sit and chat. At the end of the night, when the music was finished, we chatted some more and even had a cheeky kiss. From then on, we continued to meet each other every night, until the end of my holiday.

In the disco most nights, were Liz and Paul, a couple who had already been very good friends with Richard for many years. Paul became best man for Richard at our wedding in 1978 and Liz is still one of our closest friends today. Liz has gone on to have 3 beautiful daughters, the eldest who is now living and working in Ibiza. Another one of her daughters got married on the island and we were extremely fortunate to be able to attend the wedding, given Richard's health condition at the time.

Trip to "PACHA"

I would meet Richard some nights after he had finished work, but one night stands out for me. He said it was his night off and he was going to pick me up and take me somewhere special. How funny to think about it now, as romance has never been his strongest point, something I was to discover during our many years together.

He picked me up at the hotel in his Mum's car, an old Renault 4, with a funny gear stick, that you pull and twist to get it into gear. He then whisked me off to Ibiza town, in what I am sure was his romantic way and to the club PACHA. In the late 70's, PACHA was the place to visit, be seen in and the club that everyone talked about.

For Richard, this was fascinating, as he would love to look at the competition and see how they put it all together. I am not sure he could compete with their level in a small local disco, but he was able to absorb the surroundings, the sound, the music, the whole thing. I wasn't bothered about the technical side of things, it was nice just being with him and I felt I was able to have a little independence for myself. He made no excuse that his mind was more interested in the set up in the nightclub. The music systems, the speakers, the whole atmosphere that he was trying to take in. He would chit chat with me and make small talk, but I knew the date was mostly about him experiencing the vibes from the club, than being with me. However, I must have been happy with the arrangement and it didn't feel like a problem in any way. Afterwards we went for something to eat in Ibiza town. I remember our time together being simple, easy, and fun, but most of all laughter, what could be seen as the perfect holiday romance.

On another occasion, we had been out together and were quite late back in. My dad who had waited up, gave me the biggest telling off as I had kept my mum up worrying where I was. I was on a curfew after that and had to be in by 11pm. I didn't understand at the time and thought it was so unfair. After having 4 children of my own, I now totally understand the worry that my parents would have felt that night. We have had a fair experience ourselves of waiting and worrying about our own children returning home after nights out, so I know full well the anxiety that goes along with that.

I managed another couple of holidays to Ibiza in 1977. Cala Llonga always felt a safe and comfortable place to return to, time after time. Richard was still working in the same disco as the previous year, and we continued to meet and see each other. I'm not sure that I ever thought this was anything other than a holiday romance, but I did feel incredibly comfortable with him. He was a bit crazy and very funny, so it made it all seem light-hearted and casual. His catch phrase at this point was, "Imagine what beautiful babies we would make," I am sure exaggerating his continental accent. "What kind of chat up line is that?" I replied, laughing at him. I thought it was a nice thing to say, but never thinking for one minute that we would go on to marry each other.

On returning home to the UK, we continued to write to each other. This was the nicest and easiest way to communicate. He returned home to Holland in the winter, so I had been right about the Scandinavian link of sorts. His grandad had died, so he had gone back for the funeral. It also gave him the chance to catch up with his 2 brothers and the rest of his family, who all still lived in Holland. Richard wrote to me in English, this must have been difficult, but he did make a big effort. Some of his letters were quite funny to read, due to his broken English and spelling, but it was certainly better than my attempt at the Dutch language.

I carried on with my pursuit of becoming a cabin crew member. I was lucky to be offered a place with Monarch Airlines in 1978, based in Luton. Richard and I were still writing to each other. He asked if it was okay to come over and stay with me, as he had to purchase new music for the next season. It would be ideal, as I was living not too far from the record stores in London.

These were the days when I would ring Richard from a local phone box, using coins to speak to him and the same for Richard in Ibiza. The conversations would often end abruptly as we would always run out of money, or the line would just be cut off.

He came to stay on two separate occasions. We had a great time, going into London to buy the records he needed, just spending time together, eating out and most of all laughing a lot. I shared a house with three other girls, who also worked for Monarch, I think Richard thought he had struck gold when he realised this. It felt crazy, as we had only known each other for such a short time, but there was definitely something happening between us.

It was on his return to Ibiza that he called me that night. I could tell he had too much to drink, but he said, "Please will you come over and live with me, I really love you and want to marry you."

I had wanted to get into the airlines since I was 14 and had now succeeded, only to be tempted to give up that career, move to Ibiza and be with Richard. I had always said that I would never marry anyone who smoked or had a beard. Of course, Richard smoked and had a beard of sorts. The impulse to join him in Ibiza was immense, I was completely comfortable and happy when I was with him. After some deliberation, I decided it wasn't such a bad idea.

I didn't feel at home in Luton and hadn't settled, like I thought I would, away from Manchester. I also remembered the three months I spent working as a nanny in Madrid, which was a fantastic experience, but I was too young, at only 17. I didn't stay long as I became homesick, unsettled, and felt very isolated where I was living. Could this happen again? It's impossible to think too much about it, but my decision to join him in Ibiza was made quickly and easily. I have, however, never regretted a single day since making that decision. I couldn't imagine any different life than the one we have together, especially the great family, and as he said, the beautiful children we have made.

Apart from my job, I was young, with no ties, so felt it was an adventure and at 19, it was one I wanted to take a chance on. My parents were obviously concerned and saddened that I had given up my job after all the years I had talked about getting a position with an airline. However, they were very supportive as they knew the place I was going to be living, I believe that would have made things slightly easier for them.

They had only seen Richard a couple of times, when he used to whisk noisily through the village on his motorbike, with no helmet on, the freedom that was allowed back then. I am not sure what opinion they formed if any at all. When I asked my mum later in life what her thoughts were about Richard, she said she felt comfortable after meeting him and his mum and didn't have any real concerns for our future. That was nice to hear.

I gave my notice to Monarch and moved out to Ibiza at the beginning of the season. When I arrived at Richard's home, I could not believe it. It was the most amazing villa I had ever seen. It had the name, "Casa Siempre Bien Venidos" which means, "House where you are always welcome." The most beautiful sweeping staircase, with Mimosa and Bougainvillea trailing alongside, brought you up to the front door. To the side was a lovely terrace area, where you could sit and look out to the stunning hillside and the pine tree-covered mountains of Cala Llonga. All or any of my fears of where and what I might be arriving to, were unfounded.

Richard's mum, Christina, was more than welcoming considering she had never met me before. I wasn't sure about how much Richard had shared with her about our relationship, but if she had any concerns, she certainly didn't show it. The Dutch are such an easy-going nation, who can be very direct and to the point, but also extremely accepting and welcoming of anyone or any situation. Something I have now shared, with the friendships we have with my Dutch brothers and sister in laws and their children, who all remain in Holland.

I discovered his mum not only lived on the island too, but worked in the hotel reception, where I had stayed on my previous holidays, however, I didn't realise this at the time. I must have spoken to Christina many times when she was working, without knowing she was his mum. I don't remember Richard telling me this, or even if he did.

Richard carried on working as a DJ by night and in the local beach bar by day. He was lucky if he got an evening off and pretty much did an 18-hour day every day. I did a little promotion work for the disco and at night I would help collecting glasses and washing up. I hadn't gone out to any work so this was helpful in earning a bit of money, but Richard had assured me I would find something.

If Richard had a little free time in the afternoon, we would go off to Ibiza town to buy a few more records. He would put headphones on and listen to the new music available, which is how DJs picked their records back then. We also bought flowers to give out to people on the beach and help promote the disco. I always loved that time we spent together and could appreciate how hard he worked.

As well as wanting to get married, we both wanted to start a family, but didn't expect this to happen so soon. By the time my parents had arrived on holiday, I was already pregnant. I was working in the local laundry at the time, it was so warm I fainted and that's when I decided to do a pregnancy test. I can remember being frightened to tell my parents this news, as I wasn't sure how they would react. They took it very well and we joked about more holidays for them in Ibiza.

Richard was now 22 and after living in Ibiza since he was 16, had learnt a lot about life in a very short time. Although he was a bit crazy, he had an old head on him and could talk about anything, having quite serious views about lots of subjects. I'm sure this also stemmed from the way he had been brought up in Holland, I felt my mum and dad could appreciate these qualities.

Christina met up with my parents, they got on well with each other, so that helped enormously too. My dad, Stanley, was a bit of a charmer, always wanting to test his knowledge of different languages. Christina loved this quality and they got on like a house on fire, as she was fluent in English, Dutch, Spanish, and German. At this point I didn't know very much about Richard's dad, Guus, as he was called, only that he had left the island and gone back to Holland for business reasons.

Wedding

We tried to get married in Ibiza, but at the time the paperwork was complicated because of our different nationalities. We decided to wait and marry in England at the end of the season. We returned to England at the end of October and within two weeks we had arranged the wedding and set the date for 24th November 1978. It was an event in our lives that turned out to be the simplest, but loveliest of weddings.

The service was held in the church I had attended as a child. We were married by the vicar who was still there and who knew me very well. He was somewhat unhappy to the point of being annoyed that Richard wasn't wearing a tie. He confirmed that Richard was the first groom he had married, who wasn't wearing one. Richard hadn't even worn a suit before, so getting him dressed up in anything other than a pair of jeans wasn't easy – a tie was a step too far.

Today we wouldn't need to give it a second thought that I was pregnant. However, back in the 70's, I was worried about what our local minister would think. This was something I didn't need to be, as he was charming and lovely about the whole event, even mentioning our expectant baby during the service.

Lorraine was my bridesmaid and the best man was Paul, Richard's good friend from Ibiza. The service was followed by a reception at my parents' home, with outside caterers coming in to set the food out while we were at church. Richard's mum, auntie, and brother managed to travel over from Holland, it was perfect. We both say we wouldn't change anything about the day.

Our First Arrival

Our first son Kristian or Kris as we sometimes call him now, was born in Hope Hospital Salford, in March 1979, close to my family home in Worsley, Manchester. I waited for my six weeks check-up, before joining Richard in Ibiza. As it was a new season, Richard had to return to work, soon after Kristian was born. It seemed like the longest wait, until I was able to join him. I was so happy when at last, I could fly out. My parents came with me for support and of course, enjoyed another holiday too.

Initially we lived with Christina in the villa, but we then managed to rent an apartment for the rest of the summer, from some friends we knew, and this worked out well.

The following summer of 1980, we rented an apartment from Richard's boss, set within a village complex on the hillside. We made home as best we could and it was nice to have a place of our own for the season.

It was during this summer and when I had just found out I was pregnant with our second child, that Kristian became quite poorly with sickness, he was only 16 months old. At the time, the hospitals in Ibiza were perhaps not the best for medical problems, but certainly not the worst either. As Kristian wasn't improving, we decided to see a private doctor. The doctor advised us to give Kristian sips of cooled boiled water made from vegetables. This would help to keep him hydrated and to avoid him vomiting anything back up. He wasn't allowed to have any milk or solid food and I was so worried about him, but eventually I was able to re-introduce these. The hospitals in Ibiza, since then, have improved considerably, as we discovered several years later, when Richard's Mum was poorly with cancer. She was looked after extremely well, especially during her last few weeks of life.

It was during this time, we decided we needed to put down some roots. Maybe the medical side of things had scared us both a little. We were able to save quite a bit during the summer, but in the winter, a lot of the money was used up on living costs, to manage through the winter months. This was common for many workers in Spain, who were normally employed between April and October only. We did look at buying a property in Cala Llonga and even considered building on top of Richard's parents' home, but to no avail. Mortgages were not easy to obtain then. We looked at a house for sale behind Richard's mum's house. We approached the bank but couldn't manage to secure a mortgage with them. We came to the decision that renting was not a permanent option for us anymore.

We discussed what had happened with Kristian's illness and the difficulties we had faced in trying to buy a permanent home, deciding it would be better to try and settle in the UK. At the end of the summer season, in October 1980, we returned lock, stock and barrel to England. My parents came over with a trailer, to help us drive our belongings back to the UK. It must have been quite a journey for them, driving on the other side of the road through Spain and France, having to negotiate a trailer as well.

When we arrived back in England, we lived with my parents at first in Rotherham, South Yorkshire. My father had re-located from Manchester, due to a change of job position.

Jenny, our second child, a daughter, was born at the Rotherham District General Hospital in December 1980, we felt so fortunate to now have a boy and a girl.

Our First Home

After applying for several positions in the retail industry, it wasn't long before Richard was offered a job as Bar Manager in a new hotel. The hotel had just opened in Rotherham and was only 5 minutes from my parents' home.

We had enough money saved for a deposit on a house, so began house hunting straight away. We found a lovely two-bed town house, in a small village called Bramley, just outside Rotherham and still within walking distance of my parents' home. The house was £13,000, but even with our deposit, we needed more income to allow us to secure a mortgage. Richard went to speak with his boss and asked him for a pay rise of £10 a month, fortunately his boss agreed. It was brilliant to have our first real home since we were married.

Once we had moved in and settled, we were still able to return to Ibiza on holiday. We only needed to buy a flight and then stay in the family home with Christina, which greatly reduced our holiday costs. We also managed to get over to Holland for breaks to see the family and for weddings and special occasions. These days were particularly memorable times and in many ways life seemed a lot simpler when the children were younger. One trip we just woke up in the morning and said, "Let's go to Holland," jumped in the car, drove to Harwich, caught a ferry to Holland and turned up on the family's doorstep at 3 o'clock in the morning. They still joke with us about that now.

"Let's Have a Pub"

My parents had retired early and both had itchy feet to do something else. They kept discussing the prospect of going into the pub industry and would we be interested in this, considering Richard's skills in the business. As soon as there was any glimmer that we might be interested, my parents started on a hunt for the right property. We went to see quite a few pubs, up and down the country, some more suitable than others.

In February 1984, we moved to Wybunbury Cheshire, to run a busy and thriving local village pub. It was a challenging time as the children were still young, but we did have the support of each other as a family. It was also a great opportunity and great choice of location, living in such a lovely part of the world.

Richard was brilliant in this kind of work always giving a hundred percent to everything he took on. With the difference in ages and personalities, between the four of us it did work well. Mum and I operated the food side of things, as well as supporting the bar. My dad was chief communications and hospitality person. He was fantastic at sitting at the end of the bar, chatting to people, remembering their names, and just making customers feel welcome.

We enjoyed the experience and built up a nice business, becoming good friends with a lot of the locals, having some fantastic theme nights and occasions to remember.

After 2 years, the novelty of running our own pub, working seven days a week, was wearing off with all of us. We started to feel there were never any real breaks, even though we did share the chores and try to give each other much needed days off or cover for holidays. Whoever thinks running a pub is easy, think again.

Mum and dad started to go for days out, re-visiting North Wales, which is where my grandparents had lived for many years. They started looking at houses and found their perfect home in that area. We put the pub on the market and a sale was agreed in February 1986.

We stayed locally in Cheshire, buying a house in the next village, as the children were both attending the local school and we didn't want to disrupt this by moving further away. The house we bought was on a new housing estate in a lovely quiet village called Hough, just a couple of miles down the road from the pub, we loved it as soon as we saw it.

We moved out of the pub in February 1986 and just before we left, I discovered I was pregnant again. Our second son, Niki, was born in October, at Leighton Hospital Crewe. We named him after the famous Formula 1 racing driver Niki Lauda, but deliberated over this name for quite some time, as I was unsure about it. However, in later life we are so glad we kept it, as we think he suits his name perfectly and now just uses Nik.

Shortly after Nik was born, I met my new neighbour, Sandra or (Sandy) as I call her. Sandy had just moved into the house next door and came round to see me and our new baby boy. What a great friendship we made and still have today over 36 years later. Although we no longer live next door to each other, we try to catch up as often as we can.

Back Onboard

It was a few years later, a friend mentioned that getting to Manchester Airport was now easier, via the M6 motorway. This was due to an entrance and exit being added at junction 16, northbound, entering from the Crewe side. This made the commute to the airport more viable. I started to think that maybe a return to a position with the airlines was possible, even though it was almost 10 years since I had worked for Monarch.

I began by looking at which airlines were recruiting, only applying to those that operated out of Manchester Airport. I was fortunate to be offered a temporary position with Dan Air in 1989. I continued working for this company for three summer seasons. It was common with some airlines to offer a contract during the summer season only. I felt incredibly lucky to be able to return to the job I had always wanted to do, at the age of 30, but most importantly, being able to manage this alongside raising a family. It was a perfect scenario, working in the summer and having the winter off. If I did a very early flight in the morning, Richard was able to do the school run and I could easily be back to pick the children up and have tea on the table. Richard was always supportive of me working and the extra financial help it gave us. He also did his fair share of the childcare, where possible. I believe this was another reason our relationship has worked so well.

In 1992, I was offered a position with Caledonian Airways, part of British Airways and a long and short haul airline. I was questioned at my interview how I would manage the post with three children, something that wouldn't be allowed to be asked today. Richard and I have always respected each other, with a shared home/work life balance and we didn't feel this would be a problem. I must have assured the team interviewing me of this.

I stayed with Caledonian for 7 years, travelling to the most amazing places. I even took Jenny, our eldest daughter who was 14 at the time, for a weekend to Florida. She had to take the Monday off school and her teacher didn't believe that she had been to America for a weekend. I often flew at weekends, so between us we worked out a good system and with the help of a lovely childminder.

Our Dream Home

In 1994, we moved to a bigger house, remaining in the same village we had come to love so much. I had gone past the house so many times and thought how much I would like to live there. The estate agent told us about the house coming on the market during a visit to value our own home. He persuaded us to view it, but I told him straight away, we wouldn't be able to afford it. He must have known how I would react about the house because as soon as I saw the garden, which was huge, I absolutely fell in love with it and didn't really need to see any more. The garden was incredible, although at the time, didn't have very many plants, or borders and most definitely needed some love. With a bit of effort over the years, it has become my haven, where I am able to spend my time reflecting on the many situations I have been faced with. It pushed us to the absolute limit with the mortgage and at times, I don't know how we managed to scrape through some of the financial tangles we found ourselves in, but we did.

We sold our old house to a lovely couple, Helen, and Eddie, who met at university and were buying their first home together. Helen and I have got to know each other so well over the years, sharing lots of events with each of our families and she is still a close friend today.

A Late Arrival

In August 1996, our second daughter Katie, or Kate as we call her, was also born at our local hospital in Crewe. We called the other children down to tell them the news, after first discovering I was pregnant and they all said, "Oh no, what have we done now?" Our reply was, "Well actually it isn't what you have done, more what we have done." Their reply was, "You're not pregnant are you mum?" I had joked about having an extra bedroom in the house when we moved in and even said that one of them could be the baby room. How true was that!

After having Kate, I had to return to work earlier than I would have liked because of financial reasons. I found it difficult to leave her when she was so little. Although I had changed to a part-time short haul contract, the airline occasionally asked me to cover a long-haul trip, giving me very little notice. Things seemed to have changed for me, with the worry of being called out, I began to experience panic attacks. I felt I was no longer enjoying the job that I had been so fortunate to do for the last 10 years. I wasn't sure how we were going to manage, but I knew I would find something else to keep our heads above water and I handed in my notice.

I had a little bit of time out, but due to the financial implications, I took on various part time cleaning jobs, childminding, and healthcare positions to earn extra money, ensuring all the jobs kept me in and around our local area. I also managed to complete a part time Access to Higher Education course at a local college, to enable me to consider other options, as Kate got older. Richard was having to stay away a lot more during the week for his work. It seemed ideal timing and important that one of us was around to carry on running the home and be there for the children.

Sister (Laura)
April 2004

In January 2003, we had just returned home from the funeral of Richard's dad who had passed away suddenly in Holland after suffering from a stroke. The phone rang and it was my sister Laura, she asked me if I was on my own and able to talk. I can remember the call so well, immediately going upstairs, to be more private. I was muddling things through in my mind what she was about to tell me, but I could hear the anxiety in her voice, so knew it wasn't going to be good news. Laura had been told she had stage 3 breast cancer and was going to start treatment immediately by having a mastectomy, followed by radiotherapy. Why do we remember these moments with such clarity? At other times we can't remember what we did yesterday.

Laura hadn't had the easiest of lives, managing to raise 2 boys as a single parent. She had also lost her eldest son, Barry, our nephew, to cancer (melanoma), when he was 23. It's unimaginable to know the heartache she suffered from his loss.

I wanted to see her straight away and talk about things, but most of all, give her a hug. She didn't want me to drive to Warwick where she lived, telling me it was too late to come over that day. Laura said she had done all her thinking already and had made her mind up about everything.

Laura was very strong-willed, I can remember her having many arguments with my dad over things they didn't agree on, when neither of them would give in. I think her determination on this occasion was very much needed. I respected her decision and why she didn't want to see me just yet, even though I still wanted to go. The other side of her personality was generous, kind, and sensitive, with a wicked sense of humour. If we were on the phone together, we could be on for an hour or more, as she could talk forever. I always had to make sure I allocated enough time for a phone call and used to sometimes sigh, if it was Laura, as I knew it was going to be a long one. How I miss that now.

It was a long 16 months of surgery and treatments to try and cure the cancer but sadly, we lost my lovely sister in April 2004.

Her younger son, Mark, is an absolute credit to her, having such incredible strength, something he must have needed to get him through the years that followed. Mark is now happily married and together with his beautiful wife Abi, has three amazing children and I know how much Laura would be incredibly proud of them all.

As for my mum and dad, I am not sure how they, or any parent, manages to recover or get over the loss of a child and a grandchild. There's not a day goes by that I don't think about her. Laura is truly missed as a sister, but most of all a friend.

By the time Kate was settled in school and the other children were getting older, in 2004, I took a part-time job in the Newborn Hearing Department, at our local hospital. The job involves testing babies' hearing, very soon after they are born and is based on a post-natal ward. In 2010, I was offered the position of Local Manager for the team, which I did for 7 years. However, as things became difficult in my personal life, due to Richard's ill health and caring for both my elderly parents, I took early retirement. I later returned to a hearing screening role, which enabled me to reduce my hours and have a better work life balance. I am still enjoying this job today and think it is one of the nicest positions to have in the NHS, with a fantastic supportive team around me, who have most definitely kept me going through the good and the bad times.

CHAPTER 3

Richard

"She wants me to play Barry White."

Richard's life journey began in Holland, where he was born. He was the middle son of three children who grew up in Den Helder, a small navy town in the province of North Holland.

His parents owned and ran a taxi business in Den Helder for several years. Richard can remember all the three brothers being looked after by Auntie Rikie as she was called, whilst his parents had to run the business. Auntie Rikie used to cycle every day to their home to make breakfast for the boys and then send them off to school. Many people cycled in Holland and continue to do so today. Some carry on wearing the traditional clogs of Holland or (Klompen) as they are translated in Dutch.

The holidays to Ibiza for Richard's family began in 1969, when Richard was 13. They would travel from Holland and rent a house, in Cala Llonga, for the whole of the summer. In those days, the beaches were almost empty and the sea was crystal clear. One year, Richard took his best friend along with them. They would snorkel from dawn till dusk, spending all their days outside, on the beach, or swimming in the sea.

His parents must have fallen in love with the Ibizan experience. Over the years of continuing to return there for holidays and loving the place, they managed to buy a piece of land and had a house built. This gave them, along with other family and friends, many years of joy and happy holidays for years to come. In the late 60's and 70's it would have been easier and more affordable to purchase land for building and in 1972, "Casa Siempre Bien Venidos" became their home in Ibiza.

The same dream today would be so expensive and out of reach for most people. Ibiza has become the home to the rich and famous, which has made prices soar. It is still seen as the place to be and attracts people from all over the world for its laid-back lifestyle and vibe. We always joke that we would love to be able to buy back the family home, but then realising it would be totally out of our price bracket now.

Leisure time in Holland, particularly in the winter, would often be spent on a pair of skates, it wasn't uncommon for the canals or lakes to completely freeze over in the winter. Fishing, swimming, and boating were just a few of the many other activities that people could take part in during different times of the year.

If it was cold enough in the winter, a special event would always take place. It consisted of the eleven cities ice skating tour, in which you were able to skate from city to city, all of them situated in Friesland, with a total distance of 200 kilometres. This was open to anyone who wanted to take part and an amazing tradition. Even the King of the Netherlands took part in 1986, skating under the name of W.A van Buren. In recent years this hasn't happened, possibly due to global warming around the world, with the last one taking place in 1997.

In the summer, days were spent on the 7 kilometres stretch of beach and sand dunes in Den Helder, which runs all along the coast. It was a great place for children to spend time during their long holidays from school. The sand dunes are huge and a good shelter and potential sea defence for the town.

Christmastime in Holland is a great time for everyone, especially for the children, but they do celebrate differently to us. Sinterklaas (Santa Claus), is celebrated on 5th December and gifts are exchanged with the children. Fun things and events are organised for families, in each of the towns in Holland. The 25th December is the religious celebration just the same as in England.

The foods they enjoy at Christmas are also different to ours. Speculaas is a cinnamon spice mix biscuit, available all year round, but even more so at Christmas. They have a lot of marzipan products too. The children often receive a chocolate letter made with the initials of their name. Similar to the children in England, they also put a sack at the end of the bed, in the hope it will be filled with lots of treats and goodies. It has been nice over the years to celebrate the two types of Christmases with our own children and we have a picture of all our grandchildren by the Christmas tree, each with their chocolate letters. Another lovely connection with Holland for them all to share and learn about.

Richard and Sport

Richard was a keen sportsman, who got involved with several different types of sport. He played for one of the local football teams on Sundays in Den-Helder and loved being in goal, claiming that he was quite a good goalkeeper. However, one week he didn't turn up for practise, as he had gone off to enjoy his other hobby of motorbike scrambling, the manager dropped him from the football team because of this.

Scrambling was one of his favourite sports, although his mum told me she couldn't watch him, for fear that he might crash or fall off at some point. We can understand this firsthand when a friend, who lives in our village, told us her story of losing her son Matt, in a tragic motor cross accident. She was then approached by the organ donor team, something I will share later.

Richard played for a basketball team every Saturday afternoon, from the age of 11. His parents were kept quite busy, between running a business and looking out for the boys, with all their various activities. In Holland though, most children would get to where they needed to go on their bikes, this gave them much greater freedom and independence. Richard tells me that he was the one who always got the secondhand things. He was the middle child, so felt he never got anything new for this reason. He remembers Willem, the eldest brother, getting a new motorbike and Hans, the youngest brother, also getting a new bike. Certain memories, or sibling rivalries stay with you and are usually raised later in life, then used as evidence in an argument between each other. He now, however, has a fantastic and very humorous relationship with both of his brothers as they all have cracking personalities. They speak English perfectly, which is helpful for me, as my Dutch is somewhat limited, although I can understand some of the conversations.

Another hobby and pastime for Richard in Holland was fishing. Either going on the canals in his spare time and school holidays or, going fishing in the sea. In his early years, Richard belonged to a fishing club, but as he got older it became something he could do on his own, or with his friends. When we spent our 2 years running the pub in Cheshire, he joined the local Wybunbury Anglers fishing club. The fishing club had all their meetings and ran their HQ from the tiny snug area within the pub. This was how Richard was first introduced to fishing in England.

During the summer months, he goes to a lovely spot just down the road from us, to sit and relax. Since his heart attack, he bought a motorised trolley to enable him to transport his fishing gear without too much difficulty. This allowed him to spend more time with the hobby he loved and helped improve his mental well-being. I'm not into fishing at all, but I can totally understand the pleasure and relaxation it offers. On the couple of occasions, I have helped

Richard take his equipment and set it up, I have been able to experience the beautiful, peaceful surroundings. It has been a good escape for him to be able to gather his thoughts.

Some of our children and now grandchildren, also took up this hobby over the years. All of them became better and extremely competitive at winning fishing competitions than Richard, much to his frustration, with most of them getting their names on the fishing cups. On the plus side, it must have been his teachings and patience that helped them achieve this. They all still try to wind him up, that they are better at fishing than him

Holland to Ibiza

In 1973, Richard had just finished Technical School in Den-Helder, with a Diploma in motor engineering. It was at this time that his parents decided to move to Ibiza permanently. They sold the family taxi business and made the move over.

His dad always travelled by car, he didn't like flying and avoided this at all costs. Driving gave the family a good opportunity to transport any belongings or new things for the house as they could take these with them by road. Any bigger items would have had to go by van. His dad would always drive from Den-Helder to Barcelona. This would take around a day and a half covering a distance of 1600 km. He would stop only to take a short break, or a quick shut eye, arriving in time to take the ferry to Ibiza.

All three brothers would travel with dad, but his mum would fly out earlier, to sort things out in the house for when dad and the boys arrived. At the port of Barcelona, they would board the car and passenger ferry to Ibiza, usually a night ferry. The crossing would be another 12 hours. The same ferry journey has since been reduced to about 8 hours travel time. I think Richard's mum had the right idea travelling by air, this would have been my choice every time.

When his parents decided to move out to Ibiza permanently, Richard at 16, had just completed his education in Technical

School, so it seemed to be the right time for him to move also. His two brothers remained in Holland. Willem was already working, and Hans was in his last few years of education. Hans remained in the care of Auntie Rikie and Auntie Alie, another great aunt who also helped look after the boys. The aunties had a house together so Hans continued to live with them, until he was able to complete his education. Both Willem and Hans still visited their parents, making full use of the long summer holidays to go out with their friends and spend time with their family. It must have been great being able to holiday in Ibiza whenever they felt like it.

His parents rented a bar in the village of Cala Llonga, which they ran together. Richard used to help in the bar to give his parents and other staff a break at siesta time. Most bars and shops in Spain would close between 1 o'clock and 4 o'clock in the afternoon, due to the heat of the day, or to have a rest or siesta time as they call it. Richard's parents chose to keep the bar open.

He also secured a job as the DJ, in one of the local hotels. This was seasonal work with rarely a day off for anyone and was the time that everyone needed to make their money. He used to get about on a motorbike or moped, the best and cheapest way many people got about on the island.

During the winter season, when the hotels and bars had closed, Richard would get some extra work if offered, helping an English contractor maintaining apartments. The apartments were situated on the same development where we had rented one previously.

After a couple of years, a local businessman offered Richard a job as DJ, in another disco situated in the village of Cala Llonga. By this time, his parents had left the bar as his dad had returned to Holland and his mum was working in the reception for one of the hotels. Richard's additional job during the day was working in the beach bar, from 11 o'clock in the morning, till close, usually around 6 o'clock in the evening. He would then go to work in the disco, starting at 10 o'clock at night, often not arriving home until 5 o'clock in the morning. They were long working days but essential to make a living.

I knew when he had finished work as he had bought himself a VW Beetle. I could hear the roar of the engine, revving up the steep hill that leads to the apartment we were renting at the time. The car was his pride and joy, after he had taken it to the local mechanic, who did a magnificent job of respraying it to a fantastic burnt orange from its previous pale cream. I was usually getting up with Kristian as Richard was just coming in to go to bed.

The recollection of Richard's side of the story, when I asked if he would play Barry White, is somewhat vague. There were lots of guests who he would meet over the year and Richard says he can't remember this occasion. How can I blame him? It was a fleeting moment back in 1976, when I was only 17 and he was 19. However, when our paths crossed again and Richard was in his new DJ location in the village, he says he does remember me coming up to him. The only reason he remembers this is because his thoughts were, "She's a bit of all right." I would like to think quite attractive would have been a nicer description. He admits he did fancy his chances though. At least our versions of the story match and as they say, the rest is history.

Beach Bar

During our first season together after having Kristian, I would walk down to the beach in the afternoon and spend a couple of hours with Richard, whilst he was working. If I didn't do this, we would see very little of each other. We attached a baby bouncer to the beams of the beach bar, this allowed Kristian to jump up and down on the sand and watch everything going on around him. Richard's work colleagues at the beach bar, Pepe and Cristobal, used to love playing with Kristian and keeping him entertained in between serving customers, this gave me a little time off from baby duties.

Cristobal, Richard and Pepe in the disco 1979

We have since lost touch with Pepe, but we know that he now lives and works in Tenerife. We will definitely try and visit him one day. He was a very funny guy and always went back to his home in mainland Spain in the winter, to harvest the olives from the family business. Pepe used to tell us long stories about this and the difficulties of managing and maintaining an olive farm. Cristobal and his wife Carol remain great friends to this day. They have continued living and working in Ibiza and have a large family of their own. Each time we travel back to Ibiza, we always catch up with them and share our news of each other's lives like we have never been away.

It was down on the beach one day that we met a couple who have also remained lifelong friends. Mavis and Derek came up to the beach bar and Mavis asked for a cup of tea. Richard didn't quite understand how she wanted her tea made, so I intervened to help with this. It seems amazing how you can meet people in this simplest of ways, then remain friends for a lifetime and it all started with a cup of tea.

It turned out they lived right next door to Manchester Airport, in Cheadle, Cheshire. In later years, we made lots of visits to see them, leaving our car at their house if we were going on holiday and flying from Manchester. Derek would then taxi us to the airport.

They became like second parents and the best of friends with us. They never had any children of their own, Mavis said it just didn't happen. However, they had been together since they were 13 and had the most amazing, loving relationship. Sadly, Mavis lost her soulmate, Derek, to cancer in April 2011, just a few months before Richard had his heart attack.

Languages

Richard's use of languages is incredible. Whilst I can get by with my broken Spanish, Richard like his mum is fluent in Spanish, English and Dutch. In fact, his Spanish seems to flow more easily than his Dutch. His brothers laugh at him when he is searching for some Dutch words, this isn't surprising as he has been away from Holland for so long. Our children also take the mickey out of him with his continental accent, especially when he is saying the names of the F1 drivers because he can pronounce their names correctly.

The teaching of languages in Holland seems to be more productive, with all the children learning English in school. The English TV programmes remain in the original English language format, with no dubbing. Dutch subtitles are added to assist with the translation. This helps the Dutch learn English more easily as they are hearing it as it should be, with no changes. The two ways of learning English must be an advantage for a student, as by the time they leave school, they have become extremely proficient in being able to converse in that language.

Settling in England

On our return to England, Richard was fortunate to find work quickly and in an occupation that came easily to him, as Bar Manager, in a large hotel in Rotherham. When Richard was short of staff, he would ask if I could cover a few shifts for him, I was more than happy to help. It gave us time together, even if it was in a working capacity. We were still waiting for our house purchase to complete in Bramley, so I was able to earn a bit of money and my mum and dad were on hand to help us with the babysitting.

We stayed 2 years in Rotherham and during that time, Richard was transferred by the same company, to run a wine bar, in the centre of Sheffield. The hours again were long and unsociable, with many late nights. He was responsible for locking up after a shift and I was always glad to see him arrive home safely, something we had to accept for anyone working for the pub industry.

In some ways it was a relief to move to the pub in Cheshire, this felt like a safer option for us all to work and be together as a family. It was clear early on that Richard was the main driving force and energy that was needed to keep it going. He made great friendships, especially with the fishing club members and many others in the village, as we all had. Bank holidays used to be absolutely heaving, together with some of the fun nights we used to organise. Christmas and New Year were another busy time. Richard's brother and sister-in-law came to visit us during early December. This was great for them to experience an English pub at its best and a nice way for us and the children to celebrate Christmas the Dutch way.

After 2 years, we all knew that our time at the pub was coming to an end due to the long and demanding hours. After acknowledging this, Richard started to consider his options for alternative work. He was in the process of trying to start his own business, as a stocktaker for the pub trade. He purchased a small portable computer and created his own stocktaking programme with the intent of working for himself. However, he realised early on it would take some time to create a client base and to secure an income, so he decided to apply for other jobs.

By the time we had moved out of the pub, he had attended several interviews with different companies. He was offered a position as a stock controller with Grand Metropolitan. The company owned the restaurant brand, Berni Inns and the job also included a company car. It couldnt have come at a better time. We met Mark, who was the Stock Control Manager for Richard in his Berni Inn days and had originally interviewed him and offered Richard the job. After considering our options and taking into consideration the time it would take to build his stocktaking business, it seemed sensible to accept the job offer with Grand Metropolitan.

Mark and his family have gone on to become very dear friends, with Mark becoming godfather to our youngest daughter Kate. Mark and Richard hit it off from day one and we have shared so many laughs on work trips and social events. Mark sends me Valentine's cards every year, pretending they are from someone else. He has such a crazy and fun personality, with a great sense of humour. In some relationships, this could cause jealousy, but isn't the case with us, or for Mark's lovely wife Melanie. Mark remains an incredibly caring person, who has sent so many supportive messages throughout the difficulties we have been faced with over the years, we can never forget that kindness.

SOLD
"Casa Siempre Bien Venidos"

During the time we had settled back in England, Richard's mum would occasionally come over to stay with us during the winter months. It was during one of these visits to England, Christina announced she was going to sell the family home in Ibiza. I don't really think any of us believed that this was really going to happen and none of us were sure of the reason. Christina never discussed her financial situation and we didn't ask, so it may have been that things were becoming too difficult for her to manage. We all discussed why we didn't pull together and hang on to the house or help Christina out. At the time, we all had mortgages of our own and young children, so an impossibility for any of us to help out financially. It was sad, but we still carry such a lot of happy memories made in the Ibiza family home.

DAD (Guus)
January 2003

In January 2003, we got a call from Holland to say that Richard's dad Guus, had sadly and quite unexpectedly passed away on his own at home. He had suffered a massive stroke, which is particularly sad. Guus had always said to the family that he never wanted to be alone when he died.

We travelled to Holland for his funeral and met up with all the family. Richard hadn't seen or spoken to him in recent years or before his death. We didn't visit Holland as often as we had done previously, when the children were small, mainly due to the cost of travelling. His dad never managed to come over to England, even though we asked him many times. We put this down to his fear of flying or driving in England on the other side of the road, which wouldn't have been something he would have liked to do. However, it was still his dad and that alone brings all the memories back after losing someone so suddenly. The children and the grandchildren all laid a rose on his coffin, it was a very sad moment.

My thoughts were mostly for Christina, who was also there. I know she still had a soft spot for Guus, especially after all the years they had spent together. It reminded me of how difficult it must have been for her, when I first arrived at the villa to be with Richard. During that time, she knew that her marriage to Guus was over and that he never intended to return to Ibiza, but she kept it all to herself and hadn't even told Richard.

Richard continued to work in the same job, but over the years, the companies he had been working for were either reorganised or sold several times. Each time was a concern that he may lose his job. Fortunately, things always turned out okay. However, in 2007 during one of these changeovers, Richard decided to opt for voluntary redundancy, there were so many uncertainties happening within the company. This was a little concerning, we still had a young family and a large mortgage, but it seemed to be the best option at the time.

We were on our way up to Scotland to complete his last job with the company. Kate and I were travelling with him, the company didn't mind if you occasionally took the family along and it was nice to be able to have a couple of days away. Kate and I would go out and spend time together in the day and then meet up with Richard at night for dinner, after he had finished work. His role had changed at this point to auditor and stocktaker. It was while we were driving that Richard got a call from an ex-colleague Jenny, who was the audit manager for Regent Inns. She had heard via the smoke signals in the trade, that Richard might be looking for work.

Jenny offered Richard a position with her company during the phone call, with a better salary and still including a company car. She asked Richard to give it some thought and get back to her. What was there to think about? Richard was getting a redundancy package from his old company and moving on to a new position within a week, working for someone he knew and trusted. We felt so fortunate and Jenny was a great person, who had known Richard for many years. This meant that Richard would be working again with another ex-colleague and old friend Neil, who was already in the company. It felt like the auditing team were back together. Richard continued to work for the pub trade, travelling the country, doing more driving, which included many overnight stays due to the large area of the country he and Neil now had to cover.

What is Wrong with Him?

The first indicator that something may have been wrong was that driving became increasingly difficult over long distances. He started to travel more frequently by train, which helped with the way he was feeling. Jenny, who was still his manager, was extremely understanding and allowed him to continue to travel by train, even though we had a company car sitting on the drive at home. If the job was getting done, the company were happy.

One evening though, when he had decided to drive to work, Richard suffered an incident on his journey home from Lancaster, he began to feel quite unwell. He was fortunate enough to be nearing a service station on the motorway and pulled off.

He doesn't remember very much about it, but felt awful, dizzy, faint, and nauseous. We do believe now that this could have been his first heart attack, although he had no crushing chest pain, or pain radiating down one side as the medics often describe a heart attack to consist of. Richard managed to come round enough to drive himself home, how he managed this, we don't know, but he did get home safely. From then on, he knew that something wasn't right. What we didn't realise is how bad things were and what was about to happen when Richard's health really did take a turn for the worse.

He saw and spoke to several of our GPs the next day and over the coming weeks. He had to take several weeks off work as he wasn't feeling very well at all and was incredibly tired. Conditions such as Labyrinthitis, Meniere's, and hearing loss were the sorts of possible causes mentioned, but after testing, nothing was diagnosed or confirmed.

Richard went to see a Neurologist to assess his balance and possible causes for the dizzy feelings. We were able to cover this privately as he still had health insurance through his employment and he managed to see a specialist within a couple of weeks. Nothing came from this, only suggesting that Richard may be depressed and need a course of anti- depressants to see if this would improve his overall well-being. He refused to believe this was a possibility of the cause of his problems. He is not the sort of person to feel anxious or depressed and he didn't feel this was helpful in getting to the bottom of what was really happening. He was left a little frustrated that no one seemed to understand the symptoms he was trying to describe.

On most of the occasions when Richard began to feel unwell, he was often driving. This is possibly why the medics might think he was getting anxious and this in turn, was making him feel dizzy and a little disorientated, almost like a panic attack. Whenever this happened, he always felt the need to stop driving or didn't feel comfortable behind the wheel. If we were going anywhere, many times he would pull over or just stop the car and say, "You will have to drive I can't do it at the moment."

When he eventually returned to work, he would limit himself to driving short distances and if possible, chose to go by train, which his company were still willing to support. This helped enormously with Richard being able to continue working, although he still had days when he felt exceptionally tired and didn't always feel okay. In his words, not feeling unwell, but something just wasn't right.

Nothing could prepare us for the events that were about to happen.

CHAPTER 4

The Heart Attack

"Mr. Lamens you have had your Last Cigarette."

It was Friday 22nd July 2011, my sister's birthday. We drove to Leamington Spa, to visit the place where Laura's ashes were scattered and to spend some time in beautiful Warwick where she had lived.

The day had gone without incident. I had driven, as I mostly did now for longer journeys and we had taken my mum along to share the memory too. We visited Hatton Craft farm near Warwick, another place we enjoyed going to with my sister and our children, when they were all younger.

On the way home we popped into the local pub for a quick bite. I'm not sure if Richard was feeling okay at this point. He wasn't too keen on stopping off to eat, but none of us could face the thought of cooking when we got in, so decided it was the best idea.

The next day was Saturday, I was on shift at the hospital, so I was up early and ready to go to work as normal. I brought Richard a cup of tea in bed before I left, he told me that he didn't feel too good, adding," That bloody pub has poisoned me I feel awful."

He did look pale and said he felt a little sick but was okay. I thought it was likely to be an upset tummy and nothing more. How wrong was I! I can't think too long about that moment because I didn't stay with him, but Richard never wanted any fuss when he felt unwell. "Just go to work, I am fine," he said. However, if I had stayed, we will never know if his prospects and the damage done to his heart might have been very different, something I have constantly had to push to the back of my mind.

Later that morning, I got a call from our daughter Kate, saying that her daddy didn't feel very well. Richard had told her if you call anyone you should call 999. I knew that wasn't something that Richard would say easily. I asked Kate to stay with her dad, I then called 999 from my work.

Kate told me afterwards she got a call back from the 999 call handlers. They asked her to make sure her dad was upstairs and lying on the bed. They also told her to put any pets away in another room and make sure the front door was open. This must have been alarming for Kate, as she was only 14 at the time. My good friend Sue, who I had called from work, arrived quite soon after this, so she wasn't alone.

The paramedic called Kate upstairs and told her that her dad was having a heart attack, at which point the phone went, it was Nik her brother. Nik didn't know anything about his dad at this point, he had just called by chance for a catch up. The minute Kate heard her brother's voice, she broke down and frantically told Nik what was happening. Seeing Kate's distress, Sue took over the call and explained things to Nik in more detail.

When the paramedics arrived, Richard remembers them saying to him, as they were reading the ECG results, "Why have you left it so long mate," at this point shoving an aspirin the size of his palm in Richard's mouth, telling him to chew on it. There must have been alarm bells ringing for them.

Richard had no crushing chest pains, no pains radiating down one side. He just felt like he had a bad case of indigestion and thought this was caused by the meal he had eaten the night before.

Due to the severity of his heart attack, it was a miracle that he had stayed conscious. I was told later, but can't remember who told me this, that Richard had been talking all the way to the hospital, this was usual for him, no matter what was going on.

I couldn't believe that after all this time of him feeling unwell, had now resulted in a massive heart attack. Even though I didn't want to acknowledge what was happening, everything suddenly made sense. The difficulties over the past couple of years all started to piece together and why he must have been feeling the way he did.

Jenny and Kate travelled to the hospital together. Nik our youngest son, arrived with his future wife Kelly and took me up to the hospital. We just managed to get there as they were taking Richard to theatre to have a stent fitted, to clear the blocked artery. This had been the cause of his heart attack. A stent is a small mesh tube, used to hold open and widen a weak or narrowed artery, which then allows the blood to flow more freely. He was dazed by the medications they had already given him. I managed to say a quick word and tried to make a joke about what he had been up to, then quickly told him I loved him before Richard was taken off to theatre.

It felt like such a long wait until he returned from theatre. I don't think it was, it all seems a bit of a blur now. All I can remember is sitting together as a family in the waiting room. The children were trying their hardest to distract me from thinking anything bad was going to happen to their dad. I felt like I wasn't in the room with them. When I saw Richard after the procedure, he looked dreadful. The surgeon spoke to him and said, "Mr. Lamens you have had your last cigarette today, 23rd July 2011 as you have no room for another heart attack." Those words still stay with him today.

Smoking and High Cholesterol

Richard tells me he smoked from a very young age. It was later in life when he discovered he had the genetic type of high cholesterol (clogging up of the blood vessels) inherited from his mum. He was having a routine eye test with his optician, who advised him to visit his GP. People with high cholesterol can have white circles around the pupils of the eye and this can be an indicator of high cholesterol. His mum's eyes did show white circles, quite prominently and it was the same for Richard. I have since asked all our children to check their own eyes for any early signs of this. Richard tried to stop smoking and seemed to do well at first, but with all the driving he was doing, it proved a difficult habit to break. I used to get mad with him for not being able to stop, but at the same time realising I had no idea about smoking, its addiction, how it makes you feel and the difficulties in trying to stop.

It must have played a large part in the problems that were about to surface for him, but something that was now too late to change. The high cholesterol is a condition that if caught early enough, can be reduced, or controlled. With the use of statin medication and eating a healthier diet, as well as exercise, most people can try to slow and prevent a heart condition from occurring, but the condition of hereditary high cholesterol itself cannot be cured, but it can be reduced.

Richard has never suffered from high blood pressure and has never been overweight at any time in his life. However, between smoking and his hereditary form of high cholesterol, this must have been the catalyst to cause his severe health problems. Smoking can make your LDL (low-density lipoprotein) cholesterol, (the bad kind) stickier, this clings to your artery walls and clogs them up.

On many occasions, Richard had tried to give up smoking previously, to no avail. He knew this time he had no choice, after everything that had happened over the last 18 months. We now knew the real reason Richard had been feeling so terrible.

Richard spent only a short spell in hospital, just a few days after his stent was fitted. The words of the junior doctor who discharged him were, "Go home and carry on living your life." The doctor mentioned that some people can recover quickly and return to work after three weeks, whilst for others it can take much longer. Little did we know how bad the damage was, or how it had affected his heart, obviously the doctor who discharged him didn't know either.

Once at home he looked dreadful, his weight had dropped again, he was very grey in his face and he had a terrible pain in his chest, called pericarditis. Pericarditis is an inflammation of the lining around your heart. It can cause a sharp pain in your chest when you breathe in deeply or lie down. This was making Richard feel horrendous, as well as the aftermath of his heart attack.

Our local GP came to visit and see how Richard was doing overall. After the GP explained about the pericarditis, we did start to believe that he would recover from this event over time and continue with a healthier life, now a stent had been fitted.

A few weeks passed and Richard returned for several more checks, an ECG (Electrocardiogram), MRI (Medical Resonance Imaging and an Echo (Echocardiogram) at the Royal Stoke hospital. He wasn't feeling very good at all, his weight was falling and fluid around his body increasing, especially around his ankles.

With Richard's lack of improvement over the next few weeks, we decided to see a private cardiologist at our local hospital. The consultant told him to climb the stairs and exercise more. When Richard said he was out of breath and it was difficult when he did this, the consultant replied that most people get out of breath if they climb a flight of stairs. This was not the reassurance or outcome we were looking for. We couldn't help feeling that there appeared to be no hope in getting some improvement for him.

Before discharge from the Royal Stoke, Richard had been referred to the Cardiac Rehabilitation team at our local hospital. We asked what they felt the outcome was for Richard and the reply was, "You have the heart of an 80 year old and you will need palliative care." Whilst this was on reflection, a fairly accurate statement, it could have been delivered a little more sensitively. Richard hadn't even come across the word palliative care and afterwards, I had to explain what this meant. I found myself playing it down a little so as not to alarm him too much, or myself. We both didn't know what to think about any of it.

Richard had been discharged from the Royal Stoke into no man's land and we felt quite anxious about what lay ahead. As this was happening during the summer holiday time, it appeared that every doctor or consultant was on annual leave, which meant we couldn't get any answers. It was so frustrating, but we knew there was something still very wrong.

It was fortunate that we kept pushing for some answers. After chasing up his follow up appointment to review his MRI scan at the Royal Stoke, Richard was seen by one of the cardiac doctors. The doctor went through the results with us and it soon became clear, there was some concern over how things were at this point. The swelling of his feet and discomfort that Richard was still experiencing, should have started to reduce, if there was nothing else to be concerned about. We left the hospital and the doctor we had seen followed up his concerns with his consultant. This resulted in Richard being called in the next day to be admitted to the Royal Stoke Hospital. He discovered later that he was now under the care of an amazing cardiology team. These health professionals are most definitely one of the many reasons that Richard is still alive today.

After his admission to hospital, Richard met the consultant, who came to chat about how things were going. Whilst he was talking, he gently put his hand on mine. In the consultant's words, "Richard, I am very worried about you and I am glad you are here, you are in a very bad way."

Of course, to hear those words was a shock, but at the same time it felt comforting after all this time, knowing that something wasn't right. Suddenly you are talking to a professional, who not only understands, but who is taking on board the circumstances and acting on them. Richard and I were both affected and very emotional about the information we had been given, but at last felt he was under the right care and we had found a ray of hope.

He had been prescribed a high dose of water tablets to reduce the fluid in his body, this alone was putting an enormous strain on his very weak heart. He was also fitted with an ICD (Implantable cardioverter defibrillator) This device works by emitting electrical pulses which can regulate any abnormal heart rhythms, especially if these could be dangerous and cause a cardiac arrest. The device is quite a costly procedure and needed authorisation to proceed, but we were told that we didn't need to worry about this. They wanted to fit the device without testing it, this would have been the normal practice. Scans had shown that Richard had a small blood clot around his heart, it was this reason why testing the device was not an option. This could have disturbed the clot and caused other complications. He remained in hospital for a few weeks, until his fluid overloaded body became reduced and the risk and strain on his heart became less.

During the time Richard was in hospital, we were told the goal for him being under this team was that he would eventually need a heart transplant. His heart had suffered so much damage during the heart attack, it had put him in the acute heart failure bracket. Even though it was difficult to accept the prognosis given, we felt a huge amount of confidence in the team around us.

After leaving hospital, he became an outpatient under a team of health professionals that ran a clinic called "The Shine Clinic". The team provides an outpatient service for anyone suffering from heart failure and they manage a patient's condition on a daily basis. This includes monitoring his fluid overload, checking his ICD, and redressing this area, which was still quite sore. Richard had lost so much weight, especially around the ICD and chest area, you could see the device protruding just below his shoulder. However, this vital medical device was most definitely needed.

This incredible medical team were a group of professionals, who became our friends and who we trusted to deliver the care that Richard so definitely needed. We felt fortunate to have found the right pathway and even started to believe that Richard may have a chance of survival.

The Shine Clinic, a service provided by the Royal Stoke University Hospital, is in our opinion, second to none, with the team offering lifesaving support and monitoring, in the most caring of environments.

JENSON

It was while Richard was in North Staffs, that our grandson, Jenson, who was 18 months old at the time, became very poorly with an extremely rare strain of Bacterial Meningitis. He was transferred from our local hospital to Alder Hey Children's Hospital, in Liverpool, where he remained for quite a while. This was the most difficult time for our daughter Jenny and son-in-law Richard. All this was happening at the same time her dad was in another hospital, being treated for his severe heart failure. Remembering this brings tears to my eyes, with the level of strain that the whole family was under.

We managed to muddle through, with the help of family and friends, especially Nik, Kelly, Kris, and Max, who looked after our other grandchildren. Jenny and Richard (Jenny's husband) stayed with Jenson at Alder Hey. It was such an awful time and one that left Jenson completely deaf from the infection and illness he had suffered.

He has since been fitted with Bilateral Cochlear implants. This has enabled him to learn to communicate again, although it has taken an incredible amount of hard work from his parents and school input. Jenny and Richard have also learnt sign language. They are amazing and inspirational at communicating with Jenson this way.

At the same time, my mum was offered a date for the hip replacement surgery she had been waiting for during the last year. She was offered a bed at our local private hospital to carry out this operation. The timing couldn't have been worse and we discussed whether she should go ahead, but mum was determined to get this done. It put another enormous strain on myself and the rest of the family, it was just too many things to juggle.

Richard understood how things were and never made me feel guilty if I wasn't able to get to the hospital till later, or if at all. I would turn up at his bedside and just sob sometimes. From the emotion of everything, including carrying on working, it was becoming overwhelming, I felt torn in every direction.

Some amazing friends, from the church that our eldest son Kris and his wife Max belonged to, made meals for us, bringing them over on several occasions. A kindness we will never forget and such a help and support when things were so difficult.

CHAPTER 5

Left Ventricular Assist Device *(LVAD)*

The consultant at Royal Stoke completed all the necessary tests and checks to optimise Richard's condition. At this point, he was able to put him forward via a referral letter, to the Queen Elizabeth University Hospital, Birmingham. The Queen Elizabeth is the feeder hospital for cardiology patients from the Royal Stoke. This would enable Richard to have an assessment, to be considered for heart transplant. In his current state of health, his prognosis was not going to be good in the long term. The statistics show that patients only survive 12 months to 2 years, with the level of heart failure that Richard had suffered, and later we were told this was about 12% function.

In January 2012, we had our first visit to the QE hospital as we now call it, where we met Richard's cardiology consultant and his team.

As you drive up to the hospital, the view from the roundabout, situated on a slight hill, shows a spectacular view of the QE. The hospital at that time was only a year old and from a distance looks like a huge spaceship.

From day one of meeting the team, we felt that we were most certainly in the right hands and that his future looked a little brighter and more optimistic. After only two visits with the consultant over the next few weeks, he informed us that Richard's right ventricle was increasing in size. This was due to the extra workload it had to compensate for the failing left hand side. The doctor was alarmed at how quickly this increase in size had occurred.

He wanted to admit Richard into hospital for the day, to be assessed for a heart transplant. This requires a procedure called a right heart catheterisation (RHC), which involves inserting a small tube into a vein via the neck or groin and into the heart. This provides important information about the pressures in the different chambers of the heart, also the blood flow through the heart and pulmonary artery. If the pressures are too high, a donor heart would not be able to survive.

After completing this assessment, the test revealed the pressures in his heart were too high at this point, to survive a heart transplant.

There were 2 options to consider:-

1. Experimental drugs, which would be given over a period of time, in the hope that this would reduce the pressures and enable Richard to be placed on the transplant list.

2. To fit a Left Ventricular Assist Device (LVAD). This is a pump fitted directly onto the left-hand side of the heart, to assist in its function and the circulation of blood around the body.

This is when we met other staff on the LVAD team, who worked alongside the consultant. The lovely LVAD co-ordinator came to see us and to show us the equipment, explain in full what this meant and how it would affect our life. Little did we know at the time how valuable her knowledge and expertise would become in our lives, but most of all her support and friendship too.

Whilst the drugs option would be far less invasive, there were a lot of uncertainties around choosing this. If the pressures did not reduce within the timescales needed, it would not only prevent the possibility of having a transplant, but also Richard may no longer be fit enough to survive the fitting of an LVAD.

After a very short space of time – a couple of hours only, Richard decided he had no choice but to be fitted with the LVAD. I felt I needed more time. I wanted to go home and talk it through. Richard though, as always, when it comes to his own health had made his mind up. It was, after all, his body and his health. He was right of course, but for the carer (me), there will always be different emotions and concerns you don't always show at the time.

The Heart of Ibiza

CHAPTER 6

MUM (Christina)
IBIZA
April 2012

Whilst Richard was waiting to have an LVAD, we had a call from Rufino, Christina's partner, to say that she was unwell and had to be admitted to hospital in Ibiza. I have added this to the story as it is such another important link to our Ibiza life, timing and what happened after Christina's death. She had become unsteady and lightheaded and not able to stand. On doing further tests the hospital told us that his mum had lung cancer, but at the point of her being admitted to hospital, we didn't know this, or how serious things were.

Christina had been a smoker all her life. Although she too had heart problems, including triple heart bypass surgery, she was never able to kick the smoking habit. She always had a troublesome cough and we noticed this more on her visits to England to see us. This must have been a huge indicator of her illness and in the early days, we are not sure if she may have already had some underlying problems. Christina had regular checks with her doctor in Ibiza, but nothing had been detected.

There is always the possibility she knew she had cancer, but did not want to burden the family, or cause concern in any way. Something we will never know.

Fortunately, we managed to find a flight and were able to get to Ibiza to see her in hospital. We were also lucky that Richard could arrange some affordable travel insurance, given the difficulties he was having with his own health and the heart attack he had experienced a few months previously.

Richard's fluency in the Spanish language was a great help when meeting with the staff at the hospital and with Christina's partner Rufino. After seeing the consultant and talking to Rufino, it turned out that her cancer had already spread. We were told she had metastasis in her brain, which meant that her life expectancy was very short.

We flew out to Ibiza a couple of times, as the hospital called Richard twice, to say they thought she was not going to make it much longer. On both occasions we visited Christina, she seemed to pick up a little, it was nice to see her sitting up in bed and chatting. Knowing she loved the aroma, we would spray a face cloth with lavender, to calm any feelings or tension she may be having at the time. She sometimes became a little disorientated, but definitely knew that we were there with her.

Sadly, and very quickly, Christina passed away in hospital on 20th June 2012, only two months after we first got the call from Rufino. None of the family had managed to be there, but that is often how it happens when someone passes away. Thankfully, her long-term partner was by her side. She died the day after Richard's birthday and the same day in Holland that Christina's great grandson was born. We can never be sure if this has any meaning but would certainly like to think it did.

We were so relieved that we were able to travel and be there as a family for her funeral. She now lies at the top of the hill, in Santa Eulalia, at Puig de Missa Church. If you ever visit, you can look down on the whole of Santa Eulalia, with the history and detail inside the church being truly inspiring. We always light a candle in the church for her when we visit. At night, when you drive into Santa Eulalia, the church is lit up on the hill and looks spectacular. It is most definitely where Christina would have wanted to be.

Puig de Missa church Santa Eulalia

The weather as usual was lovely and warm in June, so we managed to get a little sunshine. We were fortunate to be joined by Kris, Max and their first little girl Poppy. The Dutch brothers and their family were able to travel out to Ibiza also, so Christina had all her sons on the island, this couldn't have been more perfect. I was able to book the whole family into apartments at the top of the village of Cala Llonga. It was a huge booking but worked out well. The apartments were situated up a steep hill. It would have been an impossible walk for Richard in his current state of health, so we hired a car to help us get around.

Church Service
(Christina van Halm)
Cala Llonga - Ibiza

A couple of days after Christina's funeral, we had all gone down to the beach, for a little chill out time and reflection before we were due to fly home. I popped into the supermarket, situated just behind the beach, on our way back to the apartments. In the supermarket window, there was a poster, showing the English services held in the local open-air church in Cala Llonga.

The church is a small, whitewashed building, with stone pews located inside. The floor is littered with pine tree needles, which have fallen from the trees above and umbrella the whole of the church. It is situated on a very steep hill, just at the side of a lovely apartment complex called The Pueblo Esparragos, one of which we had lived in when we had Kristian. The apartments are scattered over the hillside, allowing the most spectacular views of the bay.

It was Sunday, the service would start in half an hour, at 6.30pm. The urge to attend was immense and I turned to Richard and said, "Come on this is something we must do and a way of saying a last farewell to your mum."

We drove back up to the apartment and shouted to the others to ask if they also wanted to attend. We made it on time and there was only a handful of people, as it is such a small church area. The vicar speaking today, was the local vicar from Santa Eulalia, who happened to be Dutch, we thought this was quite a coincidence. He was with his Dutch wife who was helping him. We laughed as he was telling her to stop talking and to get on with the service.

We sang a few hymns, with the music played on a ghetto blaster, as there was no piano, no organ, and no electricity in this simple but lovely openair church. Then the vicar began. Imagine our surprise when he continued with a story he was going to share today. It was about a lovely lady called Christina, from the village of Cala Llonga, who had recently passed away in hospital.

He happened to be with her when she died and just before she did, he asked whether she would mind if he said a prayer for her. She didn't reply, so the vicar said he read that as a yes, proceeding to say a prayer anyway. We couldn't believe this was Christina's story and how moving, emotional but most of all, reassuring this was for all of us. To also know that he was with her when she died.

Richard talked with him after the service. Both he and his wife were equally amazed and grateful that they had bumped into Christina's family in this way. We came away enriched and elated, not only to have met the vicar and his wife, but to have chosen at that moment to attend the church service.

I believe the timing of Christina's death was meant to be, as a few months later we would not have been able to travel at all, as Richard was admitted to the QE to have his LVAD operation. They say things happen for a reason and that certainly was the case here. It was a blessing that Richard was able to share in his mums passing, the timing of life and death, with everything else that was happening around us.

CHAPTER 7

Fitting the LVAD

In September 2012, Richard was admitted to the QE for his LVAD operation. The surgery is an open-heart procedure, which can last between 4 to 6 hours. Some patients may have an LVAD fitted, as an alternative to a heart transplant.

Due to everything that has happened since this time, my memory of this day is somewhat vague. He had been admitted to the Coronary Care ward (CC), which we call "The Dungeons," as there are no windows or natural light. Kris was with me and I had brought a picture of Richard's mum. Later, I wished I hadn't, as I didn't want him to think that anything could go wrong, or he wasn't going to make it.

After he had gone into surgery, I drove home, thinking this was the best way to spend the time waiting for Richard, as I didn't know how long this would be. I'm not sure if this was the wisest decision, but waiting at the hospital would have been difficult too. We were fortunate to live just over an hour's drive from the QE, so this didn't feel too far away.

I got a call later in the day to say that Richard was in the ICU (Intensive Care Unit) and I was able to visit. I left home immediately, feeling so relieved, after all the hours of waiting, it was reassuring to hear he was out of surgery. When I arrived at the hospital, I was told I couldn't see Richard. He had gone back to theatre due to a bleed and they couldn't stabilise him. I decided to call Kris, who at the time was working in Birmingham, I asked if he could come over to the hospital to stay with me. I was feeling very anxious and unsure what this meant. Kris stayed with me until we knew that Richard was stable and things had settled after the operation. When we were both comfortable with everything and a lot of reassurance from the staff, we drove back home together, in the early hours of the morning.

I visited the next day and was able to talk to the staff and his consultant. The consultant explained the process of waiting for the safest time to take Richard off the ventilator. All the tubes, wires and monitors attached to him, each one doing a different role, is difficult to know or understand what they are all for, but knowing they all have a collective job. It was horrible to see Richard this way, but I had to believe he was in great hands and that this operation was needed to put him on a better pathway.

It took a couple of days until they decided they could try to take him off the ventilator. I remember Richard fighting with the breathing tube as they reduced his medications (meds) and unfortunately, on this first attempt, he wasn't able to breathe well enough on his own. They increased the sedation meds again and left the ventilator tube in place. After the second attempt to remove it, he was able to sustain his own breathing on just a small amount of oxygen.

When he was physically able to, the staff helped him get out of bed. He looked so thin and frail, but they encouraged a short, slow walk each day, to improve his mobility and strengthen his muscles. It took several members of staff, to assist with all of the equipment that Richard was attached to. It was quite an undertaking for him to walk the full circle of the ICU area. The nursing team at the QE were second to none and worked with him each day, to get him back on his feet and well enough to leave hospital. I remember no question ever went unanswered and the staff always felt like they were your friends. When Richard was moved to a general ward for his recovery, the brilliant care just continued.

It took just over three weeks for Richard to be discharged from hospital, with his recovery continuing at home. This recovery took some time. He also had to adapt to a different way of life and the new discipline he would face every day with the LVAD. I believe the recovery after an LVAD operation takes less time now and patients are discharged from hospital much sooner.

Some patients fitted with an LVAD do manage to improve the quality of their life, some even being able to return to work, but this wasn't the case for Richard. Perhaps it was his age, the stage he was at when the LVAD was fitted, or the extent his heart attack had on the rest of his body. His mobility and the speed of his movement remained the same and the tiredness was overwhelming, with some days worse than others. Learning to live with an LVAD was also quite a challenge, but we had to be realistic and grateful that this was Richard's only option to keep him alive. We can never underestimate the importance of such a fantastic device and its function, designed and fitted to patients suffering from acute heart failure and other heart related conditions. The majority of people don't know what an LVAD is and the impact it has on patients in a lifesaving capacity. The BHF (British Heart Foundation), is the best charity to gain further information on this subject and it is important to remember that everyone's experience of living with an LVAD may be different.

This illustration shows all the parts of the LVAD and where they sit on the body.

LVAD (earlier controller image)

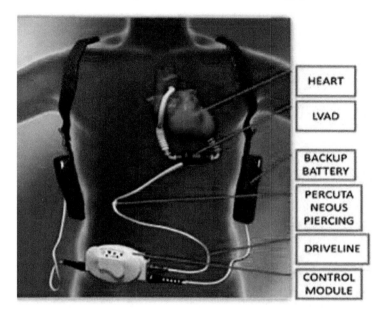

HEART	
LVAD	
BACKUP BATTERY	
PERCUTA NEOUS PIERCING	
DRIVELINE	
CONTROL MODULE	

Image courtesy of Abbott

At the time of Richard's operation, LVAD's were still in the early stages of being offered to patients. They had already been developed and widely used in America but had only just been approved by NICE (National Institute for Health and Care Excellence), to be used as a bridge to transplant in England. The LVAD is a mechanical pump implanted onto the heart, via open heart surgery. It is used for the many patients who suffer with heart failure. The mechanical pump helps the left ventricle (main pumping chamber of the heart), pump blood to the rest of the body. The pump is fitted to the heart, with the tubing from this running to the controller and sits through a small insertion, a few inches to the side of your belly button. The technical term for this is

(Percutaneous Piercing) or driveline exit, as we call it. A harness or a bag is required to be worn during the day, to carry the batteries that supply the power to the pump. These batteries last an average duration of 8 hours and are alarmed should they run below this or get near to the end of this time. The controller sits in a small pouch, this is worn on a belt round the waist.

The illustration shows the driveline exit site and the dressing required to keep the lead in place

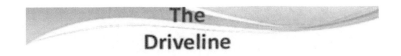

The Driveline

The driveline is internal and external. It is a percutaneous lead that connects the pump to the controller. It contains necessary power and electronic cables. It exits through the skin, on either the right or left side of the abdomen.

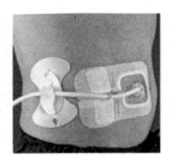

At night-time, the controller is plugged into the mains electricity, via a long cable. This is easier for sleeping because it allows more freedom of movement, although the controller will always remain permanently attached to you. A battery charger is included, to maintain a constant flow of charged batteries being available for your LVAD. The transformer is also placed in the bedroom, or close to where you sleep at night and is alarmed, should the power go off at any time. It is important that you know what to do if this happens, as the noise is deafening. If any power cuts occur in the area, this would activate the alarm to go off.

Going to the toilet during the night is somewhat challenging. You must be extremely careful that you don't pull the lead, this would cause stress on the opening to the driveline site, where it enters the body. Due to the meds being prescribed for fluid retention, most LVAD patients will need to visit the toilet frequently, during the day and at night.

For showering, a waterproof bag is provided, to place the batteries and controller, so they don't get wet. Waterproof patches are put over the driveline site (stomach), to ensure no water enters this area. A routine shower for an LVAD patient could easily take up to an hour or more. This is due to the extra measures needed to keep yourself safe and the equipment dry.

A separate black bag is given to keep spare batteries, controller, meds, and a green book. The green book includes a detailed account of all the medications that Richard or any LVAD patient is on. The book allows you to write in your daily readings shown on your controller, to ensure they are in the necessary comfortable parameters set for you by the hospital. Each LVAD patient will be set different parameters.

It is advised by the team that you should never leave home without this bag containing the extra equipment, it could be a life saver. Richard was meticulous in how he kept his book, regarding medication, the monitoring of his temperature and readings. He completed the book daily and would ask for advice from the transplant team regularly, if any changes or queries occurred. This has been a vital link in keeping Richard safe and well during his time living with an LVAD and the discipline he has maintained throughout.

However, this discipline was put to the test one evening, when we went to visit my brother in Manchester, only 45 minutes away. We went out for a meal together at their local pub. We were about to leave when Richard decided to change his batteries before the journey home, only to discover the spare batteries in his bag were flat. This meant he had very little time left on the batteries attached to the controller and we still had to get home, it was sheer panic, to say the least.

We literally left immediately, jumped in the car, and drove. We discussed whether it was worth driving to the nearest hospital in Manchester, for back up, but realised it was probably quicker to drive straight home. I considered speeding down the motorway, but if I did that and got stopped by the police, this would waste time. We drove home not speaking, both extremely tense and worried hoping that we would get there in time. We called Kate and asked her to have the two spare batteries ready at the front door for us as soon as we got home. Fortunately, we did make it and the situation went without incident, but we have never forgotten that time. We always made sure it would not happen again. Black bag, with charged spare batteries and spare controller, is the most important check, before we leave home, or go anywhere. It did prove that the battery life lasted longer than we had anticipated, after the alarm had gone off. This could be different every time and not worth taking the risk, or trying to test how long they do last, after the alarm has sounded.

When an LVAD is fitted, anyone involved in the care of the LVAD recipient (carer), must complete a short test, to understand the equipment and know what to do if the alarms go off. They are also monitored on how to change the dressings. When we returned for check-ups to the hospital, the LVAD/transplant team would change the dressing and monitor this area at the same time. This was to ensure there was no visible redness or infection around the site. It could be a simple pull on the lead, which could cause the site to open and allow infection to get in. Patients who have an LVAD, must ensure that when they are moving about, they think and navigate their activity with extreme care. It's that split second lack of concentration, when an accidental pull on the lead can happen.

Once a patient goes home, it becomes their responsibility to ensure the driveline dressing is changed at least every 3 days. This is usually done by partners or carers of the patient and sometimes by the patients themselves. It is vital to keep the area clean and free from infection, something Richard experienced a few years later. From the beginning this became my role. I used sterile packs, issued by our local GP surgery, cleaning the area around the driveline exit, before applying a fresh dressing.

In general, every LVAD patient must wait at least 6 months before being assessed to go on the transplant list. This gives time for the body to heal and recover. After waiting 6 months and completing a full assessment, it was good news, the pressures had reduced, things were going in the right direction. Richard was able to be accepted on the routine heart transplant list. There is also an urgent transplant list, but this is for patients with an extremely limited life expectancy, maybe days or weeks. Although no one could predict a long-term outlook for Richard, he had certainly been given a little bit of extra time.

After the LVAD had been fitted, we believed that Richard would receive a transplant within the first year. The device was put in as a lifesaver, but also as a temporary measure and a bridge to heart transplant. Little did we know how long our actual wait would be, as we discovered later. Many patients on the routine list often wait several years, mainly due to a shortage of donor organs. Today, there is more evidence relating to patients living with an LVAD. It can be fitted as a more permanent solution to living with heart failure, especially for patients who may not want to be put on the transplant list at all.

DAD (Stanley)
August 2013

Just when we thought things were settling down with Richard, after everything that had happened during the previous year, I was working a weekend shift at the hospital and received a call from him.

My dad had suffered a stroke and had been taken to the Royal Stoke Hospital. I came straight home and took my very worried mum up to the hospital. We met my brother and sister-in-law who had driven straight over from Manchester. Even though my dad was 89 and certainly had a good life, I was beginning to feel like I wasn't going to be able to cope with much more, knowing how much this would affect my poor mum.

It wasn't good news, dad had suffered quite a significant stroke and didn't wake or become conscious at all. He had suffered a few small TIA's, (Transient Ischaemic Attacks), or small mini strokes in the past, but he had always managed to recover well.

Dad held out for a week, but quietly and sadly passed away. Richard and I had visited him the night before, told him we loved him and that it was okay for him to go if he wanted to. We said that he might be needed up there to fix some TVs and radios, to try and lighten such a sombre moment. I knew from the conversations I had with dad, that he didn't have a fear of dying. Dad had been an engineer in this trade during his early working days and the time he spent in the army, he had been a radar operator. If there was anything electrical to be fixed, he would take things apart, draw diagrams and always be able to sort the problem out.

It is quite comforting to know he passed away the very next morning. I hope he heard us and was comforted by those words. The staff did try to call us, but we arrived too late to see him pass away.

Dad had requested that his body was donated to the Medical and Scientific Teaching and Research at Manchester University. Whilst it is difficult as a family member to consider the implications of this request, his wishes were carried out in a sympathetic and caring manner by the university. I hope dad has helped many medical students in their training, which is what he was hoping for.

CHAPTER 8

Organ Donation

A successful donor match is dependent on height, weight, and blood type. It is also dependent on the presence of antibodies in the recipient's blood that may react to the donor heart.

Sadly, over the last few years as a society, we have become less healthy and not as good at looking after our bodies, particularly our hearts. Many donor hearts that become available cannot be used, as they are unhealthy, or not suitable.

The families of deceased relatives often find it difficult to talk about bereavement. They don't always share their wish to donate their organs with other family members. This causes many people who have lost a loved one to withdraw consent at this time. At the time of death, some families cannot cope with being asked this very sensitive question. It is also difficult to contemplate the thought of their loved one's organs being used for donation, at a time when their own grief is immense.

In May 2020, the law changed regarding this process. The new law states, it will be assumed, that everyone agrees to become an organ donor after they die. However, I believe another family member can decline to allow the organs of a deceased person to be used, but the hospital would only accept this out of respect. This clarifies the importance of discussing this topic. If you are able to have an open and honest conversation within your own family, it makes things a lot easier should anyone find themselves faced with this very sad and difficult situation. If you do not agree to donate, then you must opt out by going on the Organ Donation website and click on (Register NOT to donate), otherwise it remains presumed consent.

As soon as you have been accepted on the transplant waiting list, you become very anxious and believe that a call will come at any time. When the phone rings, your first thoughts are, it will be the hospital. The team stresses that most calls to the recipient, offering a donor heart, are usually made during the night.

After 3 years of waiting, we experienced this, when Richard received his first call for a heart transplant. It was 2 o'clock in the morning and the transplant team at the QE called to say they had a donor heart. Their exact words were, "Have a cup of tea and make your way over to the hospital." They also checked how long it would take us to get there.

I raced into Richard's room as soon as I heard the phone. I very often slept in the other bedroom. Between my hot flushes of menopause, Richard trying to settle with all his equipment attached to him, having to get up several times to visit the toilet, it was difficult to get a good night's sleep, for either of us. The LVAD controller was like sleeping with a radiator, so this increased the overall temperature for both of us.

Listening to the conversation that Richard was having, I knew this was the "OH SHIT," phone call, which is what we thought we would name it. The first thing that comes into your mind, or certainly mine at the time, was that somebody has just died. Someone else at this moment is experiencing the sad loss and being asked the question, "May we use their organs to help someone else." You must quickly take that thought away from your mind and concentrate on the present moment in time.

Everything goes into slow motion. We laugh now when we think about what we started to discuss. I said, "What shall I wear for your heart transplant." Richard was saying, "Which pyjamas should I pack for my heart transplant." We didn't move very quickly and by the time we were ready to leave, the phone went again. It was the transplant team standing us down, explaining that the operation couldn't go ahead. We did find out later that the donor's family had withdrawn consent. It was a mixture of disappointment and relief all rolled into one. We stayed up talking about it for most of the night.

The transplant team had warned us there may be several calls that would lead to nothing, or false alarms for all sorts of reasons. On reflection, it was good to get that call. It was a great test, to see how we would react in that situation, should we ever be fortunate for it to happen again. It's also a reassurance that the system does work and however long you must wait, you will get the call one day.

Another account, shared by a neighbour and friend, who sadly lost her son Matt, has very kindly allowed me to tell her story. This explains the traumatic side of loss and the connection with organ donation. It sensitively tells the other side of things.

Matt's Story

Matt was a young lad who at 24, was the same age as one of our sons. He was a keen and highly skilled motor cross rider, who tragically on a race day, came off his bike and ended up at the Queen Elizabeth Hospital in Birmingham. He had sustained a serious head injury which had caused a massive bleed in his brain. They did operate on Matt to try and save his life; however, they were unable to. They informed Matt's parents that Matt was brain stem dead and that his life support machine needed to be turned off.

Before they did this and when the family were in total distress and grief, the organ donor representatives asked them if they would consider donating Matt's organs. Matt's mum says this is a question that really needs to be discussed as a family, before you are faced with that situation. It is incredibly hard to make that decision when all you want to do is bring your son home and keep him safe.

All Matt's mum wanted to do was take Matt's place, so he could live. Knowing this was not possible, she found herself running out of the hospital, to throw herself under the first vehicle she could find, as she did not want to live. Thankfully, in her head, she heard a voice saying, "You can't end your life, what about Lauren and Sean," her two other children, which made her come back to reality and she went back into the hospital.

It took over 24 hours, along with her family to make the decision about which organs to donate. This is a very hard thing to do when you are so distressed and grieving. The organ donor team also helped in this, and she says they were so understanding and helpful.

Matt's organs saved 4 other people's lives, one of which was a child. Matt's mum and his family felt very good about this. They were delighted when they received a letter from one of the people who had received one of Matt's organs to say thank you.

His mum's advice to everyone is to please have a family discussion regarding organ donation. She said she would not want anyone to be in the same position she faced, not knowing what decision to make, when you have just been told your son, or loved one, is not going to live.

CHAPTER 9

Holidays

Richard continued to have several checks each year, to monitor and ensure that things were remaining stable with the LVAD, this would ensure he could stay on the transplant list. Each time the checks would consist of a full blood count, the Right Heart Catheterisation (RHC) procedure, which measures the pressures again, followed by an ECG, and Echo. Finally, an X-ray is taken of the heart and lungs, to check that there hasn't been any bleeds or damage done during the RHC procedure.

It took a few years after the LVAD had been fitted, that we decided to take the plunge and travel back to Ibiza. Initially, we didn't believe that it would ever be possible for us to travel again but having explained our destination, the hospital team cleared us for travel. Although there were some concerns regarding an LVAD patient travelling abroad, certainly to an island in the Mediterranean, the transplant team believed the importance of carrying on living your life as best as you can, balancing out the risks associated with this.

We managed to get travel insurance and discovered the cheapest and best way to buy this was for a full year. It's essential you declare all your medical conditions and medications you are taking. The last thing anyone would wish for is to travel abroad and need medical attention, only to be told you are not covered on your insurance.

Most airlines will also carry you, but it is vital that you speak to the medical team prior to flying, to clear all the equipment that must travel with you. This includes the battery charger, all the spare batteries, the device for mains electricity at night and the massive amount of medication needed to cover your length of stay. Richard also carries extension leads and adapter plugs, to ensure we are covered for every eventuality.

It is important not to put any of your meds or equipment in the hold, instead it must remain with you inside the cabin. We use two small suitcases, both being the correct size for most airline's specifications. I carry a small bag for our passports and paperwork. Most airlines will give you an extra cabin baggage allowance for your medical equipment if you need it. Always get any cabin baggage cleared with the airline prior to travel, as this will include the Lithium Batteries.

We also book wheelchair assistance, it is such a long walk from the terminal check-in to the departure lounge and then to the aircraft. Richard's walking was slow and he had to stop several times to recover. Having a wheelchair is a massive help when going through security, it makes things a little easier using this service due to all the medical equipment we have to take with us.

I pass the suitcases through security, these are usually picked out by the staff after scanning shows the sensitive contents. Security ask for the equipment to be taken out and we are asked questions about its use. Richard is always taken to one side and scanned in a different area. It could be dangerous for him to go through the normal security scanner, this may upset the programming of the LVAD and the ICD.

It is a lot to do and does cause some anxiety, as airports are such busy places. I am always careful not to take my eye off his equipment and meds. Once you are through security, it is possible to start to relax a little and look forward to your holiday, as some of the concerns of travel are out of the way.

A nice security manager approached us once at Manchester airport and said, "Excuse me Sir, but could I just ask what all this equipment and your device is for." We thought it was brilliant that someone was so interested and not just doing their job. We hoped the information we gave may help other LVAD passengers that travel through the airport.

Most people are amazed at how it all works, but when you are travelling, people do stare and it can be quite alarming if they don't understand what they are looking at. Seeing someone in an airport wearing a harness, with two holsters on either side, could appear to be quite frightening. Richard would always wear a zipped hoodie, this helps to conceal the equipment he is wearing underneath and at the same time, is easy to take off for security to see.

Whilst travelling back from Ibiza, going through airport security, one of the security men looked at Richard and said "JODER," which translates to the F*** word in English. He took a step back and immediately called for the Guardia Civil to come over. Again, Richard's fluency of the Spanish language was extremely helpful and he was able to explain. I also carry the medical information in my hand luggage, so we can show the pictures and explanations of what all the equipment is for.

It was after this incident that we were joking that during all our trips to Ibiza, we have never met or seen anyone famous, considering Ibiza is home to many of the stars. At this point we turned round to see Jamie Oliver and his family. Imagine our surprise! I nearly said, "Hi," thinking he was a friend who knew us, then quickly realising he wasn't.

If you think too much about travelling, it could feel slightly overwhelming, but for us, returning to Ibiza, had a level of comfort and reassurance. I always joked with Richard saying, if anything terrible happened whilst we were there, I would leave him on the island with his mum, up on the hill in Santa Eulalia. On a serious note, it was a conversation we needed to have, knowing if things took a turn for the worse, I would have felt reassured in the decisions we had made together.

The flight to Ibiza is just over 2 hours, so a good start for anyone considering taking a holiday abroad for the first time, after having an LVAD. The only slight medical issue we experienced, prior to Richard having the LVAD, was during a flight to Ibiza. Due to his medication of warfarin (blood thinners), a bleed anywhere is more difficult to stem. Richard had eaten some crisps in the cabin and one had caught his gums, making them bleed, the cabin pressure added to the problem. We were never so glad to get off the aircraft and allow the bleeding to settle.

On another occasion a cabin crew member asked him to take his controller off and place it under the seat in front of him for takeoff. The controller sits just under the stomach and does look very much like a bumbag. Richard tried to explain that it was attached to him and it was a medical device. It was only when he lifted his top, to show the crew member the wires and driveline site, they believed him. We did feel a little frustrated and embarrassed as we had given all the information to the airline. We presumed a pre-flight brief would have been given to the crew regarding any passenger travelling with medical equipment.

When we arrive at the hotel/apartment room, the first most important thing to do is unpack all the electrical equipment and make sure that everything is functioning, most of all the charger. Richard will look for the easiest place to put his equipment. Only then can we begin to truly relax and unwind for the duration of the holiday. We also make sure we explain to the maid looking after the room that the equipment should never be unplugged.

We arrange car hire to make things easier to get about. Despite Richard's limited walking ability, it also adds to our security just in case anything should happen, or I need to take him to hospital. Cala Llonga is quite hilly, another reason a rental car is essential for us.

We don't do too much when we are there, as there is a level of comfort staying near the hotel or apartments. We spend time on the beach, where I can swim in the sea and sunbathe, Richard spends a lot of the time under the umbrella in the shade watching the world go by, or just reading the newspaper.

We always joke that a holiday is the only time we get chance to read a paper from cover to cover or read a good book. Richard will chat with the locals he knows, reminiscing how things used to be back in the days, when he was working in Cala Llonga. At night, we would meet old friends and eat out in our favourite restaurants. We feel extremely fortunate that we have been able to continue to travel and return to Ibiza, it's not something we would have thought possible after the LVAD was initially fitted.

CHAPTER 10

Infection

Richard managed to go through several years without compromising the driveline site. It was vital it was kept clean and free from infection. However, for one reason or another, of which we will never be sure about, the site became infected. We didn't know at the time how difficult any infection in this area was going to be to clear or control. It is most definitely one of the downfalls of living with an LVAD and very common to experience an infection at some point.

Richard was given several courses of antibiotics, to try and keep the infection under control. Whilst this treatment helped intermittently and possibly reduced the infection slightly, we believe from the medical team, it was unlikely they were ever going to be able to cure it completely, because of the type of infection he had.

As Richards carer, I continued to change his dressing every 3 days, as encouraged by the transplant team. It was clear that the infection was getting worse. The skin and wound around the site, was opening more and becoming extremely inflamed. We would occasionally take a photo of the driveline site and send it to the transplant team. From this they could assess the best course of action and treatment.

It was frustrating that we were trying to manage the infection, at the same time, knowing that it was an impossibility to clear it. We discussed what this might mean in the long term, realising at some point, Richard would probably need to be admitted to hospital, to enable the team to treat the infection more radically.

In between all of this, I got a call from my mum's nursing home to say she wasn't good. They asked me to come to her straight away. It was a beautiful hot summer's day and I had just been for a swim, something I found to be a brilliant way of helping me to relax and unwind. As I came out my phone rang. Even though I knew my mum had been deteriorating over the last few weeks, it was still a shock.

MUM (Jean)
June 2017

Since the loss of dad, my mum had slowly started to become more confused and less able to do things for herself. Mum had always had a busy social life in her early years, being a brilliant tennis player and in her later years becoming a keen bridge player. She was also good with finance and became a debt counsellor for the CAB (Citizens Advice Bureau).

As mum had been diagnosed with vascular dementia, we had no choice but to find a suitable nursing home, something I had always vowed I would never do to either of my parents. It was a decision that was taken away from me, due to the difficulties that arose with her health.

I spent the day by mum's side, holding her hand, speaking softly to her, hoping that she could hear some comforting words. I put the tennis on the TV as background noise, in the hope it was a comfort for her too. My lovely mum, sadly died, shortly after my brother arrived. I was so glad he managed to get there in time, I was sure she had waited for him.

My mum, like dad, also donated her body to medical science at Manchester University. I found this an even more difficult concept to think about, but again her wishes were carried out. I will always miss our lovely chats, her constant support, her hugs, and shoulder to cry on, that mums are able to give. The great gin and tonics she used to make me, when I popped in for a chat, or to share my worries with her about Richard, but most of all, I had lost another friend.

A few years followed, with many attempts using different antibiotics to treat Richard's infection unsuccessfully. Just as we thought, in February 2020, Richard's consultant suggested he should be admitted to hospital. He wanted to offer him a different type of procedure to try and halt the infection spreading and reduce the discharge around the driveline site. Richard went to theatre to cut open the area and expose the driveline. This would enable them to clean out as much of the infection as possible. The plan was to fit a pump called a VAC (Vacuum Assisted Closure). During this treatment, the device decreases air pressure around the wound and helps it to heal more quickly. Any excess puss or infection is forced into a dressing that has been placed over the wound.

This proved to be a disaster for Richard, within a couple of days he was oozing too much blood and had to go back to theatre, where the wound was surgically closed. He became so weak he couldn't get off the bed or go to the bathroom without fainting. Antibiotics were still the best option and he continued with these intravenously.

It was at this point, the transplant team suggested that Richard should be considered for the urgent transplant list. This would mean that he would have a much higher chance of receiving a donor organ. It also meant they were becoming increasingly concerned. The head of the Cardiology team must write to the Bristol Blood and Transplant Headquarters. They will ask if Richard could be considered, putting his case forward, with reasons stating why they feel that it is needed to move him to the urgent list.

We suspected from this decision, that if Richard doesn't receive a donor heart soon, it means his life is becoming more and more compromised by the day. The risk of the infection climbing further up the driveline and reaching the heart, was inevitable. Richard was prescribed oral antibiotics, this enabled him to be discharged from hospital. We continued to monitor the site at home and the local district nurses did home visits, to cover the change of dressings, the wound was still a large and infected area. They were a lovely team of nurses who visited him at home. It was during the Covid pandemic, which meant they all had to wear full PPE, in the middle of the very hot summer we were having, something I could empathise with, due to my work at the hospital.

It was only a few weeks later, in April 2020, the transplant team called to say that Richard had been accepted for the urgent transplant list. This again created another mixture of emotions.

I wasn't sure if I cried due to elation, fear, concern, but mainly a great appreciation for the transplant team, who were always working constantly towards the very best outcome they can achieve for their patients. This was certainly true for Richard. During the call, the team discuss if this is still what Richard wanted. Many patients choose not to go on the transplant list at all, or sometimes change their mind during the process. Richard as always replied, "Yes of course" and without hesitation.

We didn't really go on full alert, as we had when Richard had been placed on the routine list. I think we had learnt how to take one day at a time. Perhaps we had even given up a little, at the thought that a transplant may ever happen. We were also in the thick of the Covid Pandemic, so in our minds we just didn't believe it could happen.

However, in May 2020, at 2.30 in the morning, we received a call from the transplant team, just a few weeks after Richard had been placed on the urgent list. I was again in the other bedroom. I raced into Richard and knew straight away who it was on the other end of the phone. Here we go again, the OH SHIT phone call. The unreal calm that consumes you as you are taking in the information. The biggest shock was how quickly a donor heart had become available, since being moved onto the urgent list.

It was the team again saying, "Richard we have a heart for you." "If you would like to make your way to Birmingham to Ward 727, we will meet you on arrival." This time we were a little more organised and much quicker to get in the car and leave home.

We drove to the hospital in almost silence, both within our own thoughts, although I'm sure all we wanted to do was just hold on to each other. Our usual journey, so familiar for us, but taking a little less time today, as it was early morning. We have travelled so many times to the QE over the last 8 years for Richard's care and check-ups, it was just another one of those journeys, yet our feelings this time were very different.

We arrived at Ward 727 and pressed the buzzer to be let in. Initially, the nurse came to the door and told us I wouldn't be allowed to go in with Richard, due to the continuing risks with Covid. My face must have said it all, I was not going to let him go off easily for his heart transplant, without any hugs or support. After a few minutes, the ward sister came to the door and as it was confirmed that I was Richard's carer, I was allowed to go in with him. We hadn't even given this problem a second thought while we were driving to the hospital and had completely forgotten about the Covid risks.

He was given a side room and a rapid Covid test was done. This would ensure the risks were minimal to other patients and staff. Being an NHS worker, I was testing twice weekly routinely through work, so I didn't feel that I was risking anyone in the hospital by being with Richard.

Richard had all his observations done. Information was given to us about what would happen and the process from the transplant team. I think on reflection we were both quite calm and relaxed about it all. It helped again that our surroundings were familiar and friendly. We had learnt to deal with so many different situations regarding Richard's health over the years and during his care at the QE.

It was a good few hours later, I think we both managed to doze a little, when one of the doctors we knew well, came in to have a chat. He sat down and straight away said, "Look Richard, I am really sorry." At that point you know the transplant is not going to happen. The reason being is that Richard was such a complex case and had the LVAD for so long. The back-up equipment, which may be needed after surgery, was not available. This was due to the Covid impact on the hospital, ICU teams and wards with equipment in short supply. The equipment was being used for the many Covid cases being admitted to the hospital daily.

Whilst there was great disappointment for us both, there is a small side of you that is relieved again, certainly for me. We discussed this afterwards and selfishly or not, I was going to be able to take my hubby home once more. Richard says he felt the same. The disappointment and relief all flow together when thinking what we may have faced half an hour before.

The doctor thought that we had both taken the news very well and apologised for not pre-empting the situation. Richard and I agreed that whilst it was deflating, there were so many people that were dying around us daily from Covid, it was impossible to feel angry or upset about your own situation. For us, it was just another day to go home and reflect on the events that had begun at 2.30 that morning.

We carried on with life and all the Covid precautions that were necessary for Richard. Online shopping seemed a good idea to avoid any unnecessary contact or journeys away from our home. Jenny had done an Aldi shop for us. She took a picture of the products lined up in the garage and sent it to the other siblings. The quote was, "I think mum and dad are having too much of a good time in this lockdown." The picture showed mostly beer and wine bottles, it was a nice lighthearted moment.

The weather during early spring and summer was warm and sunny, this helped in many ways with the lockdown. Appreciating our beautiful garden, also allowed us the freedom to enjoy being outdoors, how lucky we are to have this! During the time of Covid, the garden had become a haven and escape where we were able to see family in a safe and distanced area.

I had to be extremely careful, as I was still working at the hospital. Every shift I had to come home and ensure that I had showered before I was able to touch or hug Richard. We are a hugee family and both found this a little difficult to start with but felt this was a small price to pay. The stories we read, of other NHS staff, the sacrifices they have made on themselves and their families, to be able to carry on working for the NHS, are all truly humbling and inspiring.

It was in June 2020, that Richard was admitted to hospital again for his driveline infection, it had become angry and troublesome. This is when the tissue viability team were involved with the care and management of the infection, with a PICO dressing that had been introduced. After two weeks, he had been discharged from hospital to the care of the local district nurses. They continued to come in to dress the area and put on a PICO dressing. A PICO dressing is for patients who would benefit from a suction device (negative pressure wound therapy). It works by helping to promote wound healing and can remove low to moderate levels of infection around the problem site. Sadly, it still wasn't improving, we needed a different plan to try and halt this infection.

Richard was re admitted to hospital. They planned to clean the area out in surgery yet again, this time, trying a different procedure using Larvae treatment. Larvae treatment is maggots of flies, these are applied to help wounds heal. The larvae feed exclusively on dead tissue, absorb, and digest large numbers of bacteria which helps to speed up the healing process. This sounds terrible and is difficult to look at, but is a proven, effective way of clearing some of the bacteria to improve the driveline site, which was vital for Richard at this point.

The site was healing well, and the hospital were preparing to discharge Richard home, he had been in hospital almost 4 weeks. This was a long time for us to be parted, particularly as I wasn't allowed to visit due to Covid. I used this as a safe time. Richard was being cared for, I could come and go to work without fear of bringing him into contact with anything I may pick up from the hospital where I worked. At least he was coming home soon, or was he?

Then the call came.

CHAPTER 11

A Donor Heart

July 2020

For Richard, the day started around 3 o'clock in the morning, when one of the transplant team came to inform him that they had an offer of a donor heart. In Richard's own words, it was the "OH SHIT" moment again. On discussing things with the team, he felt a sense of relief. There was at last another chance of getting rid and being free of the LVAD, as well as the awful infection he had been trying to fight for several years, he knew that time was running out for him. It was an instant yes for his decision, even though he hadn't spoken to me yet.

It was 5 o'clock in the morning and the phone was ringing. I was immediately on full alert, always thinking if the phone rings at that time, it will be either one of the children with a problem, or knowing Richard was still in the QE, it was going to be something important.

Hi it's me, "GUESS WHAT." It was Richard, the transplant team had just been to talk to him. A donor heart had become available and it was all looking good to go ahead this time. I remained incredibly calm during the phone call, but we both felt emotional and we could hear this in each other's voices. Richard had already cleared it with the staff that I was allowed to see him before he had to go to theatre. We were getting quite rehearsed at this.

I got up and gathered my thoughts together. Covid was still a problem within the hospital and visiting extremely limited, but on this occasion, the team couldn't be sure if Richard was going to make it through to the other side of a very difficult operation. I am sure it was for this reason only, I was allowed in the hospital. What an immense relief to hear this, it goes without saying how I would have felt, if that hadn't been the case.

I came off the phone, my mouth was dry, my mind going into overdrive with all the different thoughts swirling round my head. It's difficult to explain. Perhaps like going into shock after receiving some challenging news, but somehow managing to stay calm and focused. The difference this time was that I was on my own.

I got dressed and prepared to set off for Birmingham. I didn't tell the children due to the previous time in May, when the transplant didn't go ahead. I knew it would be some time before Richard would be going to theatre. There are so many things to check beforehand and the operation could turn out to be another non-starter.

The drive to Birmingham in our trusted Honda CRV, which has clocked up an amazing 130,000 miles, most of these accumulated by our visits up and down to the QE. I had never felt so grateful to have such a reliable car, which has never let us down. During the drive, I usually did all my thinking about how things were going and this morning, of course, had more meaning than ever. It also gave me the chance to get my own thoughts together before I saw Richard. Goodness knows what was going through his mind, whilst he was waiting for me to arrive at the hospital.

Some of the things I was thinking during my drive were –

My first and immediate thought again was the upset for the donor family. The sadness they would be experiencing right now, it's impossible to even contemplate.

Was it really going to happen this time?

Will he survive?

When do I tell the children?

I arrived early in the morning and went straight to Ward 727, where Richard had spent the last few weeks. I was met outside the ward thankfully, by one of our friendly, but most of all, familiar members of the transplant team. Richard was in excellent spirits as usual, always appearing to be in control and never showing any emotion on the outside. In some ways it would be easier if he did, as I couldn't always judge how he was coping. So far, he had always managed each challenge as it came along, as I did too. Today wasn't a good time to start changing those habits for either of us.

I remember the vicar who married us all those years ago saying at the altar, "You are marrying each other as you stand today for who you both are, neither of you can, nor should, try to change that person." Reality is very different. I know we have tried to change each other many times in our married life, but at the same time managing to emerge from any differences we have had over the years. We both tend to bicker at each other and the children laugh at us saying, "Oh they're at it again," but knowing it means absolutely nothing.

The most important thing today was that I had been allowed to see Richard before the most important and life changing operation he now faced

At last I was with him, for a long awaited, loving and very much needed hug and with both of us hiding our emotions. Staff were in and out, continuing to carry out observations most of the morning and explaining the process as things progressed. The tissue viability team came to remove the larvae from the driveline site. The team were happy that Richard was being given the chance of a donor heart, but disappointed they could not see their treatment process completed. However, they had already collected some interesting data from this procedure, which would hopefully help other patients in the future.

Richard's surgeon came to see him with his long time consultant, who had followed and supported Richard from the start. They chatted a little about the operation and how long they anticipated it would take. It was confirmed that it was going to be a very lengthy and complicated operation and apparent that just the removal of the LVAD alone would take some considerable time, several hours in fact.

It was the first time we had met the lead surgeon, who would be performing the operation. We took this as a positive sign that things did look as though they were going to go ahead. At the bedside, the surgeon and consultant carried out a scan of his femoral arteries in his groin. This was to assess the clearest side needed to insert the pipe from an ECMO machine, should Richard need this at any time, during or after surgery. ECMO stands for (Extracorporeal Membrane Oxygenation) and is an advanced form of life support targeted at the heart and lungs. It can be used in cases of acute cardiac or pulmonary failure. It oxygenates the blood outside the body allowing the heart and lungs to rest, similar to a bypass machine. His arteries have not been great for many years due to his hereditary high cholesterol and family history of heart disease. I think it was touch and go, whether they were going to be able to use the ECMO for support, after the operation. However, they decided that the right side was sufficiently clear and would be the favourite to use, if needed.

I had a bit of a joke with Richard's consultant saying, "Doctor don't you think we should have thought about this a little earlier in the day." He laughed and replied, "Yes, you are right."

I panicked a little at this point, feeling it all sounded incredibly risky, with so many things that could go wrong. I had to stop myself, as I knew from looking at Richard's face, that he wasn't going to back out now. This is what we had both been waiting and hoping for.

The surgeon checked if Richard was happy with all the information and confirmed that he still wanted to go ahead. Richard's word's and I quote, were

"Just get on with it."

The staff explained we would have to get Richard washed and shaved, particularly his chest and groin area, before going into surgery. I was glad we had something to do that would keep us both busy and as nothing can be done quickly when you have an LVAD, this was going to take some time. He couldn't shower, as the dressing from his driveline would have caused too many complications to cover and keep dry, so we gave that a miss.

In our usual methodical and careful manner, we got things done. It felt a little like I was preparing Richard for the last supper, we laughed about that. It must have been our nerves that made us both a bit giddy and silly. We got him washed, shaved and in a hospital gown, ready to go to theatre, both of us trying to act normally, but inside I knew we were muddling through our own thoughts.

I felt sick to my stomach at the thought of him going off to theatre, at the same time having a positive feeling that everything would be okay. We have talked about the situation we faced so many times previously and I have asked Richard since, had he ever felt that he wasn't going to make it, even when he had the LVAD. Richard said he never had those thoughts to a greater extent and neither did I.

It was exactly 11.30 in the morning when they came with the trolley, to take Richard down to the theatre. I can't put into words how I felt at that point. Helpless mostly, but for the first time, I did feel very alone.

We had a quick hug, I told Richard, I loved him, also telling him he was the strongest man I know, trying my very best, not to get emotional. I whispered in his ear, "Please don't dare leave me." I don't think he acknowledged anything I said, as I'm sure he just wanted to get on with it. He walked out of the room to the same lovely and familiar transplant team member, who had been there to meet me at the ward that morning and was now waiting to take Richard down to the theatre.

It was horrible seeing him go, with a very small part of me thinking, would I ever see him again, it was difficult not to. Any negative thoughts that creep into your mind, I had to push aside immediately. We knew that the odds would have been against him, for such a difficult and lengthy operation, but somehow you find the strength to believe that all will come good and he will survive this. Thinking back to this moment like I was in a trance, but I still wanted to shout, STOP, -WAIT, -NO,- DON'T GO, but I also knew I couldn't do that.

A lovely nurse came in after he had gone, to ask if I was okay and chat to me for a while. She was extremely kind. The nursing staff must be used to seeing the other side of things with patients, families and relatives who don't know how they feel or how to react in such difficult circumstances. She helped me sort through Richard's things and pack them away in his suitcase, some of his belongings would stay at the hospital until after his surgery. I packed the things that I would take home with me, then sat and had a cup of tea. I needed to stay in the room for a while, to take a moment, reflect and contemplate what may lie ahead.

It would be some time until we would know if the operation would go ahead. The retrieval and transplant team are constantly going through their checks, monitoring things, both on the donor side, to see if the heart is healthy and at the same time, ensuring Richard's observations are remaining stable too. Everything must be completely satisfactory, with all the boxes ticked, before they give the G for GO.

I gathered Richard's things, thanked the staff, then went to sit outside the lifts at the end of the extremely long corridors that make up the amazing QE hospital. On the 7th floor, which was where Richard had been, there is a great view of the outside and you can just sit and gather your thoughts for as long as you like. People watching can be very calming, particularly when you need to think of nothing for a while. I mulled over the idea of calling the children, but felt it was too soon, as we were still not a hundred per cent sure we had the go ahead. Things were carrying on around me, but I wasn't part of it and completely lost in my own thoughts.

The transplant team said they would call me when they knew it was a definite go ahead, but it could be a couple of hours at least, for all the preparation that was needed before the operation.

Richard and I have always had a connection with the church and Christianity, but we have not always engaged as much as we could, or possibly should have. However, we do believe in God and the love and strength that can be gained by believing in something much bigger than we are. The power of prayer is an incredible thing. I felt Richard was going to need a lot of prayer and support to get him through the coming days and months that lay ahead.

By 2 o'clock, I had moved outside, to sit in the beautiful sunshine we were having at the time. I was trying my best to keep calm and not to become overanxious. It was then the call came, to say it was all systems go.

I learnt afterwards from Richard, that when he was waiting to go into theatre with the transplant team, he said, "If it all goes tits up, you can use anything that's left, if it would be of any use to anybody else." Even at the last second, I couldn't believe he was able to have the selfless clarity of mind to say such a thing, when it should have been a time for his own wellbeing.

He told me that when the team came in and he heard the words, "It is G for GO," he felt everything went as fast as an F1 pit stop. Doors opened, bright lights, surgeons all gowned up and ready to go. How can we not be overwhelmed and in awe of this amazing hospital and NHS.

The last thing he remembers seeing is the LVAD monitor and the anesthetist saying, "This is not going to take long- don't worry about counting backwards from 10." Just like you see in the movies.

Later, he also told me his only thoughts of anything going wrong, is that he was confident that he wouldn't be aware of any of it. Richard had waited a total of 7 years and 2 months since going on the transplant list, to being offered a donor heart. This time the operation was about to happen.

I probably stayed for about another hour, it's difficult to even remember that now. It felt right that I stayed for a while. I was comfortable and almost reassured in the surroundings of the hospital. So many things were going through my mind. In some ways it was probably better that I was alone and I used this time to plan, how I was going to tell the children and the rest of the family. I also said a little prayer.

It was at this point that I decided to call Jenny, our eldest daughter, to let her know the events of the day with her dad. I asked if she could cascade the information to our other children. Jenny of course was shocked, elated, and emotional, all rolled into one. We carried on chatting about how crazy the situation was and of course shed a few tears together.

Richard and I had always discussed that contacting just one of the children would be the best option, if this situation ever happened. This would avoid going into too much detail which we knew would be exhausting. I would be able to speak to them all later, when we knew a little more about the operation and how things were going.

It would be hours before the team would be able to give me any update or information, so there would be nothing more to tell them at this stage. It would also be unwise to see any of the family, due to the massive Covid risks that were still on the increase throughout the country. I won't lie, that I did need a hug though, as did all our children I expect. What a strange time it was for everyone.

When I think back to getting the "OH SHIT" call from Richard, it still surprises me. It never crossed our minds and we certainly hadn't discussed it, the possibility he might be offered a donor heart during his stay at the QE for his infection, or at any time currently. With all the problems of Covid, the difficulties the NHS were facing daily, we just hadn't considered it. It was an incredible thing that was about to go ahead in the middle of the pandemic, a serious operation carrying on as planned, as though life was normal. Maybe it was better, we didn't expect it and certainly didn't have too much time to think about it. The only big difference was that I couldn't return to the hospital to be with him after surgery. It was the most difficult and almost impossible thing of all to accept.

On my way home, I got a call from my brother, David. We always speak on a regular basis, especially since the loss of our sister, Laura. He is my best friend. He makes me laugh, as on each occasion he starts off by talking about what's happening to him and or his family. It's always a long story. This time however, I stopped him and said, "David, I have something to tell you." He could tell I was on speaker phone in the car, as it always echoes a little. "Where are you?" he said. "I am driving back from Birmingham, Richard has just gone in for a heart transplant." "Oh no crumbs" he said, breaking down emotionally making me do the same. "You have made me go to pieces now" he said. The thought of his lovely brother-in-law, his best buddy, Richard, going for surgery, David found this quite difficult to take in. We stayed chatting for a while about the events of the day, it helped that I was able to share the news with him and my journey home was made a little easier.

CHAPTER 12

The Transplant Diary

Day 0

The operation began around 2.30pm. The first call from the transplant team was at 8pm, to tell me the LVAD had been removed and all was going well so far. Richard had already been in theatre for almost 6 hours, just to remove the LVAD alone. We always joked that it would be glued to him, as it had been attached for such a long time, almost 8 years.

He did need to have an ECMO machine fitted, this must have helped his recovery in the early days after the operation and most definitely saved his life. Fortunately, he didn't need a dialysis machine, another complication after this kind of major surgery, if the kidneys should fail to function. My gratitude for the team of surgeons and medics that worked tirelessly to get Richard through all of this, goes without saying, they are truly inspirational. Richard spent a total of 16 hours in theatre, what an absolutely life changing day.

It was strange times, under normal circumstances, I would either have been at the hospital waiting for Richard to return from theatre, or I would have spent the time with all our children talking things through. Neither of these options happened. Due to Covid, this wasn't possible, nor would it have been sensible. The whole country was continuing to be cautious, by self-isolating. This was now more important than ever, but how incredibly frustrating and upsetting that was to become for me over the coming weeks.

I didn't know if I might receive a call to go to Richard. If I had, it would most probably have meant the worst. I had been reminded that visiting wasn't allowed, unless it meant, end of life. I wanted to be with him so much during this time, but definitely didn't want the call asking me to come to the hospital for those very reasons. There are no words to describe my thoughts over those first 24 hours.

COMA

Day 1

Richard was moved to ICU (Intensive Care Unit) Area C, after his surgery. The team called at 9am and told me he had gone back to theatre, due to a bleed occurring. He returned to the ward at 11.30am, heavily sedated and in an induced coma. They had left his chest open, to monitor everything, this makes it easier should any complications arise. I found it quite alarming that his chest had been left open. I didn't really know what this meant, nor could I possibly imagine how he would look. For a split second, I thought maybe it was a good thing I wasn't allowed to be there, but the thought quickly vanished.

It was obviously another anxious few hours when Richard had to return to theatre. However, it reminded me of the time he had his LVAD fitted and the same thing occurred. I was reassured by this, realising it was just a first blip after surgery. Even so, I was hugely relieved when they called to say he had returned to the ward and he was stable.

Jenny had come to stay with me, as she insisted that I could not be on my own. My recollection of those first hours, during and after the operation are patchy. We stayed awake for the whole duration of the operation and also the next day. We didn't seem to be able to switch off, constantly thinking that the hospital might ring. We sat talking, putting the world to rights, trying to watch some television, anything to distract us from thinking about it all.

The hardest thing in all the time we have been together was not being allowed to visit, or see Richard, after everything we had gone through and shared. It was impossible to accept, but given the difficulties other people were experiencing, with the loss of family members to Covid, not being able to see loved ones, I was just another one on the list of frustrated people. Richard really needed me and I was losing the chance to share in the most life changing event that we would hopefully, ever experience together. I wouldn't be able to be there to monitor his care, see the changes and recovery that would be happening each day. To hold his hand, to touch, feel and talk about rubbish by his bedside, even though Richard was in a coma. These are just the normal things any partner would expect or want to be able to do.

It was during the evening of day one, Jenny told me I needed to sleep, so I did take some sleeping tablets and apparently, I was gone in 10 minutes. We had called the ward to check on Richard, before we even got through to the hospital, I had fallen asleep. Jenny had to speak to the staff. After she had come off the phone, she pulled the covers over me and told me I said sleepily, "What are you doing, trying to steal my money?" It appears that Richard and I both have a concern over money, especially when we are in a sleepy state of mind, as will be mentioned later. I don't remember saying anything at all about money, but it did lighten my mood a little when Jenny told me this.

Day 2

Richard had remained stable for 24 hours and his chest drains were working well. A chest drain is the simplest and safest way of draining the pleural space of blood, air, or fluids after surgery. All I kept thinking was that he had made it through and is still here. I had to remain optimistic unless I was told anything different.

Day 3

A settled day. There is a possibility of Richard returning to theatre tomorrow, to close his chest.

Today, I started to think how I am going to remember all that is happening on the long road of Richard's recovery, which lay ahead for him. We had been told his recovery would take much longer than most average heart transplant patients. This was due to the length of time Richard had lived with the LVAD and the time it took to remove it, prior to the donor organ being transplanted. If Richard asked me anything afterwards, when he was well enough, I wouldn't be able to tell him, because I wasn't there to see and observe things for myself. It was at this point, I decided to keep a diary of the information being communicated by the staff, when I called each day. It not only helped me to monitor how things were going, but subsequently inspired me to write Richard's story.

Day 4

A staff member called me at 8.30am, to say Richard was booked to go back to theatre, to have his chest closed. The ECMO will stay in if needed. Richard returned to the ward at 12 o'clock in the afternoon, the ward called to say he was settled.

Calling ICU, to speak to staff, always involved going through the hospital switchboard, this meant a long anxious wait and sometimes being cut off. The staff gave me direct numbers for the ward, this would hopefully improve communication for me. Prior to surgery, I was there only to see Richard go off to theatre and then I had to leave the hospital. The ward wouldn't have been thinking about giving me contact numbers and couldn't have predicted which ICU ward he would go to after surgery. It was also the last thing I was thinking about.

When I called today, I asked if it was possible to visit, but I was told straight away, this was still not allowed due to the Covid restrictions in place at the hospital. As an alternative, I asked if any photos could be taken of Richard, I wanted to see how he looked, good or bad and to have those memories stored of his journey. This also wasn't allowed, as Richard hadn't consented to this beforehand. Prior to the operation, these were all the last things on your mind. However, on reflection, it would have been nice to have followed his changes with some pictures, to realise the enormity of what he had been through and to see the improvements as they slowly started to happen.

I made a conscious decision to return to work today. Jenny thought I was absolutely crazy, but it was the only way I thought I was going to be able to cope. I wasn't allowed to visit, I couldn't speak to Richard, so it seemed the sensible and most positive thing to do, given the circumstances. If I stayed at home, I would have found it extremely difficult. I would have been over thinking everything and I had to stay strong, for when I was really going to be needed. I had a lovely job, working three days a week, with a good support team, so it was the right thing to do and a positive distraction, to help get me through the days ahead.

Day 5

Today, for some reason, I started to feel a little frantic, helpless, and frustrated. You can only act on the information you are given, but I was starting to overthink everything. Not being able to see the condition Richard was in was the worst thing. I called a good friend from the transplant team and left a message, to see if she could update me.

At 9am, I managed to speak to the ward and they were very informative. Richard had needed a bronchoscope procedure the previous night. This was to clear his lungs, due to a congestion build up after the operation and he was now more settled. His heart was functioning with support, but no more than normal support at this stage (within range), is the correct terminology.

Our friend from the transplant team did call me back, to explain things a little more. The right side of the heart was struggling in the beginning, due to the donor suffering a brainstem death. This can cause cardiovascular and respiratory changes after transplant, normally this will recover slowly. She explained why the bronchoscope procedure can be needed. Extra blood products, are given during the operation and this can cause excess fluid to build up on the lungs. She reiterated that Richard was very poorly, but remaining stable and she reminded me that he still had a long way to go.

On reflection, what was I really expecting to hear? Richard was only 5 days post major surgery and I was certainly not going to hear the words, he can come home now. I knew I needed to try and be reassured, the staff caring for him, were doing their very best every day with his care.

At 1pm, the transplant team called, it was after the MDT meeting (Multidisciplinary Team), to provide me with an update. They were considering reducing his ECMO support, in the hope that it could be removed tomorrow. Clots were still present in the left side of the lung. Richard would need an X-ray, to determine if another bronchoscope procedure was required. They would probably wait until after the ECMO was removed, to decide this. The heart was still functioning well at this point.

At 6.30pm, I called the ward. The staff told me that Richard's sats (amount of oxygen showing in the blood), had dropped to 65%. They aspirated a little blood and muck from his lungs and they came back up to 71%, which is apparently normal at this stage. I was still struggling getting used to the terminology and information being given to me.

He is okay, but it is unlikely they will reduce his ECMO just yet. They managed to turn Richard on his side to have a wash. This is a difficult procedure to do and can take up to five nurses to assist with all the tubes. It was not easy for me to visualise or appreciate the commitment of the staff in a phone call explaining his care. It goes without saying, this was the best and only option at the time. A thought goes to all the ICU team, Area C, who were looking after Richard daily and updating me on his progress.

Day 6

7am, there had been no change overnight or any more of these similar episodes occurring and Richard was quite settled.

3.30pm he had a steady day, so ECMO was reduced at lunchtime. As this has remained steady, they will keep reducing it, with the possibility of removing the ECMO in theatre tomorrow. Richard had been suctioned that morning and had a chest X-ray, which seemed clearer. I was told that one of the ward consultants had tried to call, but I had missed this, she would try again later before she went off shift. Staff assured me there was nothing to worry about, it was just a routine call to give me an update on how things are.

Day 7

I called the ward and the consultant happened to answer. He told me that Richard was going to theatre, to remove the ECMO, if all goes to plan. His levels and support would be turned down and they would wait to see his heart's response. The heart is monitored the whole time and if the heart is not ready, the ECMO can immediately be turned back up. The consultant felt confident at this time that the ECMO would come out.

The transplant team called to say Richard went to theatre at 11am. A vascular surgeon was present to repair the artery, should the ECMO be removed. Also in theatre was his cardiology consultant, who would fit a temporary RVAD (Right Ventricular Assist Device), via the neck for extra support, but this is precautionary and may not be needed. An RVAD can help to stabilise your condition and can give the medical team time to evaluate things.

We later found out, during a routine check-up with Richard's cardiology consultant, the team had devised an A to Z for surgery. They had thought of a back-up plan, for anything and everything that may go wrong. It sounded like mission impossible. It seemed they were not going to let him slip through the net, after all the years of care, toil, and investment to get him to this stage.

The staff said Richard still looks very swollen, due to the fluid overload and blood products given to him after transplant. This is reducing daily and his gas exchange had improved. Gas exchange is the biological process through which gases are transferred across cell membranes, to either enter or leave the blood. This is a continuous process that happens between the blood and cells throughout the body. The team are happy with where things are, considering the length of surgery, the assistance needed post-surgery and all the blood products he had been given.

In the afternoon, the consultant from the ICU ward called to say Richard was back from theatre and the ECMO had been removed successfully. There had been a slight incident, an episode, as the staff called it, when Richard's heart rate had gone out of rhythm. The heart was shocked to put it back into sinus rhythm. A normal heartbeat is referred to as, normal sinus rhythm (NSR). It seems quite drastic to have to shock a patient but is the quickest and most effective way to regulate the heart. The doctor said this happens to 25% of patients after this type of surgery.

The RVAD is not required at present but may be needed later. Richard needs to settle and rest now, for the next stage of his recovery plan. It was also mentioned that when they move the ventilator, he may need a tracheotomy to support his breathing, this will depend on responses and breathing at the time.

7pm he is still settled, and all is okay. Tomorrow they will look at reducing his sedation. I mentioned sending in any messages, photos, clips etc to read or show to Richard. The staff gave me the hospital link Lettersforlovedones@uhb.nhs.uk. A brilliant hospital service, especially significant during the Covid times.

This is the first letter I sent to Richard using this hospital service:-

Hi Babe,

It's me. I know you haven't heard my voice all week because of the situation, but just to let you know you have come out the other side of your Heart Transplant as you promised me and are doing amazingly well.

It's been over a week now and it's time for you to be waking and getting rid of the ventilator,---see if you can do that for me and there may even be a chance I can visit, hold your hand again and help you through this like the last few years.

I miss you so much its crazy but stay strong and use your fight to get through this and I know there will be so many more times in Ibiza for us to share together. As well as all those jobs I have lined up for you when you come home. The garden is getting overgrown so I may have to get the troops in to get some work done.

Your kids are so proud, Kris, Max Jenny, Nik, Kelly, and Kate and all those grandchildren they have managed to produce, all love you so much and we are talking daily about your recovery. (You see, it's still all about you). Willem, Yolanda, Hans and Marjan are also thinking of you and sending their love from Holland.

The neighbours, friends and family have been amazing and looked after me whilst you are away so don't worry about me.

Stay strong and I am pushing to see you every day so get those lungs breathing and you will be running very soon.

Love you forever my Dutch DJ

Shirley. Xxx

Day 8

I was told this morning that Richard had another episode where his heart rate had increased to 170 SVT (supraventricular tachycardia), this is where the heart rate can increase suddenly. He was shocked again and this regulated the problem.

He is on nitric oxide with gas/oxygen, (nitric oxide performs important chemical signalling functions in humans). This needs to be reduced first, before taking him off the ventilator. They will look at reducing his sedation, oxygen and monitor these reductions. The ward round is on, so the staff were waiting for an update from the team.

Later in the morning, the doctor called me to say Richard was stable enough to turn off the nitric oxide. This was to see how he copes, in the hope of waking him and taking him off the ventilator. The doctor had no concerns over his high heart rate episode. The drugs he had been given to help reduce the problem, should kick in and regulate this. At 5pm, Richard had been off nitric oxide since 10.30 am and had been stable, with no problems since then. His sedation meds were reduced at 1.30pm. Richard had moved his head and fluttered his eyes, but his heart rate then increased, so he was put under more sedation. At 4.30pm, he had another episode of high heart rate, so he was shocked again and was now stable.

The nurse looking after Richard's old driveline site, had applied a honey dressing on the infected area and said the wound looked clean. This had been one of the main reasons Richard had been moved to the urgent transplant list, so it was reassuring to hear that it was healing well.

Although the LVAD had been removed, the driveline site had been left open so any infection could be controlled and the wound allowed to heal naturally. The increased heart rate episodes could be because Richard still has an infection in that site. He also had an Intravenous cannula (IV) fitted, which had been in for a week and needed changing. They use this to administer or remove fluids, such as blood samples, which are needed daily at the present time. Bloods and a swab from the infected site were taken to identify any current infection. No more changes today, just rest for Richard, but they will tweak his sedation meds and reduce these slowly.

I wasn't expecting Richard's driveline site being left open to heal. I did think once the LVAD was gone, the site would be sewn up and everything would heal together. It does make sense and I now understand why they would leave this wound open. It had been a massive source of infection, which had caused many problems in the days, weeks and months leading up to the transplant. The team wouldn't want to jeopardise anything that could get in the way of his recovery and this was the routine treatment for the driveline site after transplant.

Day 9

Richard had a stable night until 5am, when one of his IV meds was changed. He had another episode, so was shocked again, to resume sinus rhythm. The ward round was now on and there is a possibility they will want to have another attempt at waking him.

I asked how Richard would feel with all these episodes of being shocked. The consultant assured me, only one shock was required to stabilise him, he also said that he would not be in any pain with this procedure. It was mentioned again, that when the ventilator is removed, there is a good possibility that Richard will need to have a tracheotomy.

It was late afternoon when I called, and he had been stable until the middle of the day, but his heart rate elevated to 170, so he was shocked again. The staff are still thinking this is related to an infection. His CRP (C-Reactive Protein) is 177 today, this had been over 200,(normal should be below 10). The liver releases more CRP into your bloodstream if you have inflammation in your body. Raised CRP levels are a good indicator of this. His temp is now 37.7 but had been 37.9 earlier. If his temp goes over 38.0, together with raised CRP levels they will suspect sepsis. The IV line in his neck was changed yesterday and sent to be tested for any source of infection.

Richard's sedation meds have stopped, in the hope that he will wake naturally. The nurse said his eyes flickered when she spoke to him and his head moved a little. If he has another episode of high heart rate, then just one shot of pain relief will be given, instead of full sedation meds. These meds can take so long to get out of the system and they are keen to wake Richard. His blood pressure did not rise after the last episode, this is a good sign.

The longer a patient is in a coma, the greater the likelihood of other symptoms or problems occuring, particularly physical disabilities. However, some people can make good recoveries, even after an extended period in a coma. These are the reasons why they are so keen to wake Richard as soon as possible.

Day 10

Today his white blood count was concerning, his temp was raised to 38,0, indicating the possibility of sepsis. His sedation has been raised slightly as he appeared to be uncomfortable. His CRP level though, was slightly down. The doctors are with him now, to discuss the next plan, but are waiting for his swab results, to identify the infection.

I was asked to call back in an hour for an update, but I found it upsetting to hear that he appeared to be uncomfortable. I know they are doing absolutely everything for him, I just want to be there.

When I called later, the staff had turned and washed Richard. He seemed okay during all of this and there was no elevation to his heart rate. The doctors are happier with his infection markers, his CRP is down to 110 and his white blood count is now 25 from 23 yesterday. This can sometimes happen when the body is fighting infection. No changes are needed to his IV antibiotics. His blood pressure remains stable and he is taking deep breaths, which is good. His temp is also reduced to 36.7 (normal). The staff have stopped his sedation again in the hope he will wake naturally, although they have indicated there is little chance of that happening today. If he doesn't wake up in the next 2 days, they will consider a tracheotomy.

What an anxious time. All I can hope and think about is that Richard isn't suffering or hurting inside. I asked if I could visit, I was screaming inside and urged them to push for me to be able to see him.

In the evening, Richard had another couple of episodes but didn't need to be shocked, his shock pads have been removed, that must be a positive sign. His sedation meds will again take a while to get out of his system. He is responding to commands from the nurse. His eyes are flickering but he isn't moving any of his limbs yet.

Day 11

This morning, the nurse asked me if I was okay to call back later, as she was busy with Richard. I did appreciate how busy the staff must be. When I called back at 12.30pm, the nurse sounded negative, saying Richard was not very responsive and may end up with a tracheotomy later today. Another episode had occurred, but he hadn't been shocked and managed to regulate himself. I asked again about the possibility of visiting and was told she would ask for me.

I understood the severity of Covid and the restrictions around visiting but was finding this more and more frustrating by the day. To receive information and updates via a phone call was not only difficult for me but was extremely time consuming for the already busy staff. It was sometimes hard to understand and translate the tone and depth of the information from the staff. The longer this went on, the harder it was going to become. All I wanted to do was be there, sit by his bed and hold his hand. I was aware of not becoming a pest to the staff and sometimes worried about even calling the hospital, often feeling guilty when I did. However, most staff didn't make me feel that way and I always felt they told me everything they could.

During my phone call that afternoon, I was told that I would not be able to visit by one of the staff. I must have been having a bad day, as I took the tone of the conversation as harsh and with no compassion. The trust policy was still the same, visitors would only be allowed, if the patient became end of life. I should have felt relieved by this, but it didn't help, with the frustration of not being able to share in Richard's pain and situation. I was told that my presence would not be of any benefit to him. I disagreed, but didn't feel at that point, it was worth saying anything in response.

When people are in a coma, or close to coming out of one, the most reassuring thing must surely be the sound of a familiar voice. I knew Richard was struggling to come back into this world and I just wanted to fight with him.

Things had finally got to me. I know there were thousands of other people going through this in the same way, due to Covid. However, when it's your loved one, it really doesn't matter, you just want to fight to be there and the only hope you have is to keep asking if it was possible.

By evening, there is no change. They are not ready to take him off the ventilator and the plan is to take him for a tracheotomy tomorrow. There is not much response from Richard, even though his sedation stopped yesterday afternoon, however, he has had no more episodes.

This was the most negative and saddest day for me.

CHAPTER 13

OUT OF COMA
A New Beginning

Day 12

Richard had been stable overnight and starting to follow commands. There had been movement of his tongue and slight movement of his hands and eyes. They have decided to take the ventilator tube out this morning and whilst there is no plan for a tracheotomy, it is still possible. His GCS movements are good (Glasgow Coma Scale). The Glasgow Coma Scale is the scoring system used to describe and detect the level of consciousness in a person.

I called the Patient Experience team to ask if the letter I wrote had been delivered, I was told that Richard had received it.

The ventilator has now been removed and Richard is breathing alone with the help of Oxygen (O2). He took a cough and a breath, truly amazing after his time in a coma, on a ventilator and the first glimmer of hope. He is still listening to commands, but not strong enough to move his limbs, or squeeze a hand strongly. The doctors want to wait a few days for Richard to get stronger before being concerned.

The LVAD site is covered with a honey dressing that is being changed every 2-3 days. Richard's CRP is below 44 and his white blood count has reduced. He may need a chest X-ray later today.

The letter I sent hadn't been opened yet as it had been quite a busy day, but staff said they would read it to Richard this afternoon.

At 9pm, the evening staff said Richard is stable. He has a large mask, with O2 and vapours. It is difficult for him to hear speech, although he is trying to communicate. They will slowly reduce the O2. How desperate I was to be there knowing it would have helped, but I also knew it wasn't going to happen.

Richard has managed to ask for water, although he is not able to squeeze a hand or move his limbs. He does have some feelings in these areas but still isn't able to move. This can be down to critical illness neuropathy (disease of the peripheral nerves), related to extreme trauma or infection. The staff think that some infection is still present in the old driveline site. The tissue viability team will return to review and check on the wound.

Day 13

I sent another letter to loved ones today. At the moment, it's the only way of trying to create some communication between Richard and myself. I know he is still not fully aware of what is going on. He is only just waking and probably feeling like he has been run over by a bus.

The second letter sent using the hospital service:-

Hi it's me again,

I wanted to let you know how amazingly well you are doing, even though you probably don't think so right now.

The hardest thing for us both is not being able to see each other and to chat about rubbish like we do, to argue and laugh at who's right or wrong. I keep chatting to the nursing staff to let them know a little bit about us so they can hopefully get to know you better. The nurse said you didn't look old enough to be married for 41 years. I said that's because you've been well looked after. (By me)

You are going in the right direction now and when they get you up, you're going to feel like rubbish - but work with those physios and nursing staff and they will soon get fed up of you and send you back to the ward. The sooner you're stronger the sooner we will be back together. Just imagine what your first shower will be like, without that LVAD. I really hope I can be there to help you.

All your family are okay and Willem and Hans too. I am talking to them daily and absolutely the whole world is sending messages of support, love, and prayers for your recovery.

The garden looks amazing, I cut the lawn yesterday. Jenny and the boys came round and brought Mitsy a new toy and she was going crazy running round the garden with it. Then she slept all afternoon because she was exhausted.

At the moment these letters are the only way we can communicate, but at least you know I am there with you. As soon as you are speaking, they can get your phone and we can speak and see each other properly, which will be truly brilliant. (That was a good move you have my old phone).

Love you forever, stay strong and work hard to get through this next stage and you will be back fishing before you know it.

Shirley xxx

The nurse said Richard was doing very well. They are going to sit him up, wash and turn him this morning, then he will be having an Echo. I was asked to call back later in the afternoon.

Richard had a busy day, as the physio team had sat him up and moved him, to sit on the side of the bed. It doesn't seem a lot but must have been a huge effort for him. His O2 supply has been changed to a tube up the nose so he doesn't have the large noisy mask-humidifier. He is speaking more and has even asked for his phone. I had completely forgotten about this, until he mentioned it. His phone had been left with his other things on the ward, before he went to theatre. I told the staff and they said they would organise someone to go and pick it up. The staff felt that Richard was very low (I'm not surprised) at this point.

At 6pm, I sent a message to his phone (I love you), for a test to see if we had communication. Then at 6.30pm my phone rang, it was Richard. Words cannot describe how I felt. I was trembling, it was incredible to hear his voice and so emotional but I tried desperately not to show this in my voice. He sounded terrible, but that wasn't surprising.

The first thing he said was, he hoped I had got the finances in order, which really upset me, I thought he was saying he wasn't going to make it. He also said that he was in a concentration camp and they were trying to get rid of him. I slowly explained how long he had been asleep for, that the staff were trying to get him better, hopefully back to his old ward and an area of the hospital that is more familiar to him. His voice was much deeper and a little strange, he sounded completely exhausted. It became apparent later, these were some of the many thoughts in his head relating to the hallucinations he experienced during his time in a coma. These would become clearer to both of us over time.

AN AMAZING DAY

Day 14

This morning Richard asked the staff to call me. What a lovely surprise and how incredible, considering he was only 2 days out of his coma. He said he feels like crap, but he was talking much better and with some of his old humour, this was lovely to hear. The staff told me that he had remained stable overnight and it was Richard who asked to call me first thing in the morning.

Richard described the area he was in as a war zone and that he wanted to come home. He didn't like it when I said he had to get better and stronger, accusing me of siding with the staff. He even said, I fancied the male nurse that was looking after him and that I was a flirt. I tried to remind him how long we had been married, to bring back some humour, but he couldn't remember.

At first, he said he couldn't remember his phone password either, but after several moments he did. I think that's amazing and shows how strong the mind is, with all he has been through and all the drugs that were still being pumped into him.

He told me the staff keep waking him up and won't let him sleep. I reassured him, saying it's because they are trying to get him better. I talked through what had happened, from accepting the donor heart, what impact the operation had inflicted on his body, it was all going to take time to heal and recover.

At this point, the staff said that his phone battery was nearly flat, and they had to go.

The frustration alone at this stage was just unbearable. I strongly believe that not being able to see or be with Richard may have played a part in his recovery taking longer. The mental state of a patient who isn't seeing a loved one, family member, or friend, must surely be affected by this absence. A phone call was my only contact with him and I must remain grateful for this, but it was difficult.

Mid-morning

On reflection, it had been nice talking to Richard and reassuring to hear a little humour and strength back in his voice. With these thoughts, I decided to pop out and do some shopping and realised I had a missed call. When I got back to the car, I immediately called him. We did FaceTime for the first time, I was absolutely amazed and emotional, to say the least, at how bright Richard looked. He certainly didn't look how I would have imagined.

The doctors were doing a ward round, so all the familiar faces of the transplant team were there. They expressed the need to get his mobility going and that he would be feeling extremely tired. One of the team hadn't seen Richard for a few days, she said she thought he looked great.

We did a FaceTime call later, but Richard was too tired by this point. He had physio sitting on the edge of the bed, whilst the Occupational Health team (OH), assessed him. His arms were moving better. A splint had been put on his legs for support and he was trying to wiggle his toes, but without much success.

One of my good friends Sandy, was with me when I called and was listening to the conversation. When I told Richard who was with me, he straight away said, "Oh no that will cost you." Sandy and I both laughed when we discussed this afterwards, agreeing how strange it was, the money thing had been mentioned again.

He also told me that I needed to pay the bill. There appeared to be great concern with him over costs and money. This will make more sense later in the story and in his recovery period when Richard remembered more about his visions and hallucinations he was experiencing from his medications.

He told me he wants to bring the staff member, who was looking after him that afternoon, home to live with us. I wonder if he's thinking at this point that he is never going to get better.

They are going to try to move Richard to a window view, for stimulation and to let him see a little of the outside world again. I asked Richard how he felt on a 1 to 10 scale, with 10 being the best and he replied 5. All things considered, I didn't think that was too bad.

He said the staff asked him if he would like me to visit and straight away, he replied "It's not allowed." I'm not even sure if this is a true statement, or why the staff would have asked him this, it was only in Richard's thoughts maybe. He must have picked up chatter and conversations around him, lying in his bed, hearing the staff say to the many relatives over the phone, there was no visiting allowed, it was almost like a child saying it.

It had become very hot on the ward and Richard was given ice packs on his head, to cool him down.

The doctor wants to leave his chest drain in and review things tomorrow.

Jenny was with me and spoke to her dad. She asked him if all the lovely nurses were looking after him. Again, Richard said, "This is going to cost you." Jenny said to him, "You seem very worried about money at the moment dad," making a joke, that mum always kept all the money. Straight away Richard said, "and you lot," meaning the children. Richard was ready to end the call after 5 minutes, you could hear the exhaustion in his voice. It was like some of these conversations were not making any sense to him either.

Day 15

This morning Richard was settled, but he hadn't had much sleep and said he feels like shit again. He had been moved to a window view and was watching the Grand Prix, one of his favourite pastimes, on a large TV the staff had provided for him. He had the ceiling fan on to cool him down.

In the afternoon we did FaceTime, Richard looked tired and didn't want to talk.

The staff said they are discussing taking his chest drain out. He asked me how he ended up like this. I felt incredibly sad that he wasn't able to realise where he was, or what had happened. His mind must have been whirling, trying to sort these thoughts out. I tried to explain again about the donor heart and how it is normal for him to be feeling this way.

He was upset as he had a poo and what a job it had been for the staff to clean this up, he was very upset about it. Saying that, he still managed to ask for his iPad as he knew the Grand Prix was on that weekend. I thought he's already over the previous toilet incident and I found this a good thought to end the day on.

Day 16

The first thing Richard mentioned this morning was the Grand Prix, even discussing what channel it was on. He said he had a nice view from his room.

The staff had put a splint on his leg, to help improve the muscle wastage that had occurred during his time in ICU and to support the weak left foot. Physio was also planned for later in the day. His heart is still functioning well and the drugs that support the heart, were being reduced daily. After the staff had explained all this to me, Richard shouted, "Okay that's enough now let's go." This meant he had enough of talking and we agreed to speak later. It's a good job I knew him very well.

On our FaceTime call later, Richard looked really good. He was sitting up in bed enjoying some ice cream. He'd had a physio session earlier and his chest drain had been taken out. They were not able to reduce his 02 yet. The staff said he can manage 5 minutes chatting with them, then he's had enough, but his mental attitude is amazing. Richard reminded me again about his iPad. I said I would arrange with the staff to drop it off for him, at the same time asking if there could be any chance of using this opportunity to see him.

Day 17

We didn't speak today until the afternoon, when Richard said he had a bed sore and it was painful. He said he was horrible to one of the staff this morning and that she wasn't going to come back in a hurry. It was confirmed that he had been given morphine to help with the pain, I wondered if this may be the reason he had snapped at the staff earlier.

When I called back later, Richard was tired after watching the Grand Prix. He had been put on his side, to avoid the pressure on his bottom. He seemed to be having a lot of interrupted sleep, they had given him Zopiclone, a sleeping tablet at night, to try and help with his sleep pattern. He is speaking more clearly every day. I asked if the children could ring him and his reply was, "No, not yet."

Day 18

I waited until the afternoon to call him. He seemed exhausted, after all the physio and recovery that must be taking place in his body. The consultants are pleased with his progress, which was good to hear. His white cell count is good and his CRP infection markers are almost in the normal range. His bed sore was improving too.

He is eating ice cream and custard in small amounts. We discussed Nasi Goreng, as the nurse looking after him today knew all about it. Nasi Goreng is an Indonesian dish, we make on a regular basis. The Dutch are very familiar with these kind of rice dishes, as well as lots of other Indonesian foods in Holland. We often cook this for the family, along with a satay sauce. This is made with peanut butter, garlic, and onions, it's absolutely delicious and goes well with any rice dish.

After a few minutes Richard was ready to go off the phone, as he felt too tired to talk. I continued to speak with the nurse who said he had an increased heart rate episode last night, but his meds had been adjusted for this. They are also monitoring his fluid overload, with increased water tablet medication. I said to Richard, I wished I could take some of his pain for him and his reply was, "I will pay for this." I'm not sure what he meant by that remark, in his semi distressed state.

He suddenly asked about the garage door. We had planned for some time to have a new automatic one, because the old one was so heavy, I could hardly lift it open on my own. We had put this on hold with everything that had happened in the last couple of months. This was a positive sign that he was concerned about the garage and that he'd remembered any of it. Also, by reminding me he had put a cross in the garage, where he wanted the electrician to position the power source for it.

Day 19

Richard called to say he had sat on the edge of the bed and in the chair for a short while. The physio was pleased with him but said not to overdo it. His nasal tube is still in place. The SALT team, (Speech and Language Therapists), had visited Richard and said he was now able to increase his solid food intake. He had managed ice cream, rice pudding and a fruit pot. Staff mentioned that he is almost ready to go back to the ward, but his mobility remains questionable, confirming this was expected and due to how poorly he had been. It was reiterated that Richard had been one of their most poorly patients. Staff said they would get one of the doctors to call me to give a proper update on his progress. I asked again about the possibility of visiting.

Day 20

I called twice today but there was no reply, I thought they must be exceptionally busy.

The doctor called me late afternoon for a catch up. They are extremely pleased with the progress Richard has made and everything is going well. Richard had been sitting in the chair for an hour, moved by a hoist, as he isn't able to weight bare just yet. He won't be able to return to the ward until his mobility improves and he is more independent. His oxygen had been turned off for a while and he was managing to breathe unaided.

The SALT team advised that his swallowing needs to improve before his NG tube, (Nasogastric), can be removed, to ensure he has a sufficient calorie intake. An NG tube is fitted to ensure a patient, who has difficulty swallowing, can receive food via a tube that is passed through the nose, down the throat and into the stomach.

The doctor confirmed that Richard had managed very well after the ECMO and ventilator were removed.

He has something called ICU neuropathy and ICU myopathy. This happens to patients who have had such trauma to their body and acute illness. It develops while patients are in the intensive care unit. It is typically diagnosed by limb weakness and unexplained difficulty in weaning from mechanical ventilation. This is common after such an intrusive operation and length of stay in bed. These conditions will improve in time and with more mobility, to help build up muscle waste.

The physios are happy with his progress so far. The doctor joked that he will be glad to get rid of him from ICU, to stop him moaning. He assured me that Richard's sense of humour is quote, "Full on, and he never stops talking." He said that his kidneys must be made of steel to come through what he had. In the doctor's words, "I don't know what he is made of." His white blood count was up because of the steroids, but this is also normal at this stage. There have been no more episodes, when his heart goes out of rhythm, since Saturday evening. The doctor reiterated they expect this to happen after heart transplant surgery.

When Richard is back on the ward, the team will do a biopsy, to ensure there is no rejection of the new heart. A biopsy is a small piece of tissue taken from the heart and tested for rejection. His driveline area is healing slowly and still being monitored by the tissue viability team.

This was a great follow up call to update me on Richard's progress. It was very much appreciated and explained to me by a doctor, who knew Richard well.

The transplant team also called to update me and explain the importance of a disciplined routine regarding medication, after a heart transplant. Richard is more than used to this, his life has been dictated by medication and equipment for the last 8 years. The team also stressed that it would be at least 6 – 12 months, if not longer, for Richard to begin to feel better, after the massive surgery he had undertaken.

I tried to call Richard later in the day but there was no reply. I understood he has so much to do now during his daily routine, to help get him mobile and get his limbs stronger and working.

Richard called me on FaceTime early evening, but his mood was low, he said he was really fed up with not being able to get mobile. Jenny was with me at the time and came into the living room and said, "Hi" to her dad, but there wasn't much reaction and Richard replied, "I'm not good today." He went on to ask if the doctor had called me to discuss things. Although my conversation with the doctor had been positive, hearing Richard's mood made me feel completely helpless.

One of the team called later, to say they had looked at the small bed sore that had formed and was causing a bit of discomfort on Richard's buttock, this was the word he used to describe the area. He was happy with the look and care of the sore and explained it was a very small area. I felt guilty, as I had asked them to have a look at this, which meant moving Richard again to view this. He was tired and uncomfortable enough already, without having to be moved, yet again. They agreed to move Richard onto his side more, to relieve some of the pressure. I think overall, it was the right decision to ask them to check on this.

I'm feeling extremely remote from Richard, with not much connection at all. He can't describe or talk through his pain and frustration on the phone. He doesn't have the energy to do so, certainly not the same as he would if I were with him. Even though it had been a positive day, relating to some great feedback on his progress from the team, for all the usual reasons, I feel so very sad, but mostly frustrated again.

CHAPTER 14

Out of ICU

Day 21

I decided this morning not to call the hospital today. I thought Richard might need some space, to not feel pressured into speaking to me, or anyone for that matter. I thought he would call me, if he wanted to, I also didn't want him to pick up on my mood. I needed to back off a little for my own sanity, to try not to overthink or worry about things when I perhaps didn't need to.

I was booked into the hairdressers for a cut and highlights. I couldn't believe how tired, emotional, and drained I felt, nearly falling asleep when Sandra, my hairdresser, was washing my hair. It must have relaxed me, as I felt so much better by the time I got home.

I decided to take our little Chihuahua, Mitsy, for a walk. Mitsy has been the most wonderful company for us both, particularly now and during Covid, she has made me go out for a walk most days. This simple exercise helps enormously in creating a positive mental attitude, it can change your mind set in half an hour, from feeling low, to things feeling okay. Every time I walked out around our village, I would see someone to speak to, all of them asking how Richard was doing. It always reminded me how lucky I was, to be surrounded by such lovely neighbours.

We acquired Mitsy, after our youngest daughter Kate, at the age of 19, decided to go and enjoy a season working in Ibiza, although we are not sure how much work she did. I suppose we only have ourselves to answer for that. Kate asked us to look after Mitsy while she was away and luckily Mitsy is still with us now. For a Chihuahua, she is brilliant with all the grandchildren, she gets so excited, wagging her tail and running up to them, whenever they come to visit.

Whilst I was out walking, the OT team called (Occupational Therapy), to chat about Richard and to find out a little more about him. This was to enable them to judge his personality, his mood and to guage where he was with his recovery. Given the previous day's communication with Richard and the hospital, it perhaps wasn't the best time to catch me to talk about him. I knew he was feeling low, but the staff had been positive with the feedback they had given me.

I assured her that he is mentally alert, although extremely frustrated that his mobility isn't returning as fast as he would like. I told her I felt very little connection with Richard, but I wasn't surprised at this, given all he is having to juggle and we weren't able to be together. We agreed that this is unnerving and upsetting. This can be a common concern after someone has had a transplant of any kind, but particularly in Richard's case, mainly due to the length and complications of his surgery.

I couldn't be sure if Richard was going to have the same personality as before. It did worry me a little. Some transplant patients can struggle mentally with the thought of a donor organ of any kind. This can sometimes cause a change in behaviour or mood relating to this. It was always at the back of my mind, but far too soon to be thinking that this was happening with Richard.

I tried to build the best and most positive picture I could of Richard's personality, to help her make the right decisions regarding his care. She said they are hoping to get Richard to sit in a chair, in the morning and the afternoon. She asked me how things were in our home, regarding the bathroom, shower, toilet and getting up and down the stairs. Also, if Richard drove a car, what type of work he did, as well as his hobbies and interests. This all stopped me for a moment, suddenly making me realise I needed to begin to think about these things. How our home might need to be changed or adapted, depending on Richard's needs when he does eventually come home, especially if he wasn't going to be able to get up and down the stairs. She finally said that Richard is still being hoisted into the chair, but she did assure me that he is making small improvements every day. The conversation left me with much to think about.

I was called by one of the team in the evening to say that Richard was being moved to Coronary Care (CC) that night, the place we had named, "The dungeons." CC is an area of the hospital that has no natural light or windows and is quite a morbid area. It has a terrible phone signal, so any calls or FaceTime are probably unlikely to work. I tried to believe that moving Richard to CC was a positive step, but with no communication possible, it was going to make things even more difficult. I wondered why he couldn't go straight back to a normal recovery ward where he is well known to the staff, this would be beneficial for his recovery. I was also concerned that he may not receive OT or physio when he was down in the dungeons and this would slow his progress. Another concern was that he would be leaving one to one care and going to an area of approximately three to one. Considering at this stage, he is not able to do anything for himself, Richard was extremely anxious about the move and so was I.

Day 22

I called a little later today to see if contact was possible by phone, but they were busy hoisting Richard back into bed.

Richard called back to say he wasn't going to CC (what a relief). He still isn't able to push the call bell or even scratch his nose, so they felt it was better to leave him in ICU, until he is stronger and his dexterity has improved. The move could possibly be another week, then he may go straight back to the main ward. I felt much happier hearing this information.

He had sat in the chair twice today, his exercises were going well and he can almost hold his phone himself. What an achievement that must feel, after so long of not being able to do anything for yourself. He said his right hand was moving better than his left.

The Patient Experience team delivered a letter today from another LVAD patient Kevin and his wife Sharon, who Richard had got to know quite well over the years. Kevin had been trying to contact Richard by ringing his phone. It was when he had gone for his own check-up at the QE, that the transplant team informed him that Richard had a transplant. It was a lovely feeling to know how many people around were thinking of him and hoping for a good recovery and I know it gave Richard the lift he needed.

The letter Richard received from Kevin and Sharon.

Richard Lamens - QE Birmingham

Heart Transplant

May be in Critical Care or Coronary Care Unit

Could you please say "hello and we wish you a speedy recovery" to Richard for us, we have got to know each other whilst both in hospital as we both had LVAD's, Richard has now just undergone a heart transplant, but I only have his mobile number and we are trying to find out if he is doing ok.

If possible, please pass on our thoughts to his wife Shirley and if she needs anything to let us know.

Many thanks

Kevin and Sharon

We had a really nice conversation and I told him I had sent some pictures of the new garage door and our lovely garden. I asked him if he was strong enough to give me a hug and his reply was, "Not yet, but nearly." It was another glimmer of humour, normality, and connection with each other.

Day 23

The staff called to say that Richard had been moved today to CC. She said that Richard was very upset and frustrated about it, but they had needed an ICU bed for another patient. I managed to speak to Richard, it turned out there was a phone signal in his bed area, this was very fortunate. As it was the weekend, there had been no physio or OT, but he said he wasn't bothered anyway. He blamed his anger on the drugs, the uncertainty about moving wards and the worry of his limited ability to do anything for himself.

Richard mentioned his iPad again, I said I would drive over tomorrow and see if I can hand it over to someone. The area he is in now has no TV or windows and most importantly natural light, so he is feeling very low, helpless and a little panicky. To balance all of this out though, each new day is a bonus, he is still here and we will get through.

In the afternoon, another staff member called, to assure me that we had a phone signal, that Richard was okay and in a lovely room, but mostly she didn't want me to worry about him. I thought this was the most caring of gestures. After talking to Richard, she was worried about me and what I would be thinking of his care in the new surroundings and situation. How kind of her to take the time to call me and reassure me that he was okay.

The nurse asked if I could bring Richard's iPad, deodorant, and shaver in. I nearly jumped off the sofa in anticipation that there may be a possibility of seeing him. We arranged for me to bring the things to the hospital the next day and that someone would meet me in reception. Richard repeated the phrase, "This is going to cost you and you are going to pay." The money situation again, but I was never sure what this meant. The nurse told him he was being horrible to me during the conversation. He then added, "With all that he had to cope with, I had it easy." It made me feel sad and happy at the same time to hear him say that, totally understanding how frustrated he was feeling. I knew there was no malice meant in what he said. Richard's personality was definitely still there.

In the evening he called again, to tell me they had found his shaver on his previous ward. We must have left it there before his transplant, but he still needed the adaptor. He sounded a lot brighter and had managed to eat cottage pie for tea. I felt relieved to hear a slightly lighter tone in his voice, but I think that had been due to the hard work of the dedicated staff, trying to pull him out of his low mood.

Day 24

I called Richard, to check if he needed anything else before I left home, we had a lovely long chat. He said he had hallucinated last night, although he couldn't remember too much detail, but it didn't sound very nice. The nurse informed me that Richard would now be going to Ward 304, as this is the next stage of the recovery pathway for a patient moving from CC. A familiar ward for him so another positive stage.

Richard is now able to hold his phone and press the call bell. I asked if it was possible to see him when I arrive with his things. I was told that it would only be people who have not seen loved ones for weeks that would be given priority and this would be very much limited. I found it very difficult to believe I didn't fall into that category.

Jenny came with me for the journey and we arrived at the QE at 4pm. We called the ward, to say we had arrived, quickly asking again if there was any chance of seeing Richard. The nurse did go away and check, but it wasn't possible, they had too many transplant patients and the Covid risks were still extremely high.

She met us in the QE reception where we handed his things over. The nurse said that Richard's mood was very up and down. He was also hallucinating and had some trouble sleeping over the last 2 days. This is called REM (Rapid Eye Movement), which could be caused by where he is positioned in CC, as there is no relation to night and day. This is due to the lack of natural light, but also the trauma he has been through. She said she will push for visiting for me on her handover and when he is moved to 304, as this would help with his well-being and mental state.

It was incredibly frustrating being at the hospital and so close to Richard, but not actually being able to see him. Inside I knew I was screaming, I don't know how I managed to keep it together. I felt slightly reassured that the nurse was going to push for me to visit and this helped. We were still struggling with the Covid pandemic, which didn't seem to be improving.

Jenny and I took a photo outside the QE, as a positive memory of our visit. It was a milestone, Richard at last was being moved to a general ward where he would be familiar with the area and the staff. I cannot imagine being in the situation that Richard finds himself in, but his mind continues to be amazing and I believe is the key to recovery in the long term. He has, however, got a long journey ahead to get his movement back, his body stronger and be able to recover from the trauma his body and mind experienced from the transplant.

Day 25

When Richard called today, he was completely fed up. He had been moved last night at 7pm to Ward 304, which is the pre-op cardiac ward, he said it was a shambles. They had tried to feed him through his NG tube at 3am in the morning, then at 7am, he was told he needed a Covid test. It didn't make any sense as he was in a side room and had continually been tested for Covid previously, but this was hospital policy.

Richard is still so completely reliant on the staff to help him, that he has become scared and frightened, suddenly finding himself at the mercy of five to one staff for care and support. It is now 25 days since his transplant and I am still battling with my frustrations at not being able to help him, or at least take some of the strain off the staff. Covid, what a nightmare it is for everyone. Richard thought he should have been transferred to a post op cardiac ward, however Covid procedures would not allow this and at this point, I don't believe it would make any difference to his care. Richard spoke to his consultant, who has shaken a few feathers to get him more support on the ward.

Later in the day, Richard managed, with the help of the physio team, to be positioned via a hoist, in the hope of being able to put his feet on the floor. He said he could feel the floor with his feet, but his toes were turning the wrong way and were still very swollen. The pain and pressure he felt was excruciating on his body. To do this task required an immense effort, it was a huge reality check to guage exactly where he was in his recovery. I must keep reminding myself how far he has come and not even 4 weeks post-surgery.

Day 26

I spoke to Richard this morning, he'd had a terrible night. He hadn't slept at all and the staff had tried to take blood but hadn't been able to do so via the normal route. One blood sample, taken by the doctor had got lost. The staff had told Richard he would need a PICC line (Peripherally Inserted Central Catheter). This must be inserted by a specialist team, so couldn't be done immediately, but is a procedure that can be performed at the bedside. A PICC line is a long hollow flexible tube fitted into a vein in the arm and sits between the elbow and the shoulder. The tip of the catheter is fed through this vein, until it reaches a larger vein above the heart. It helps the staff to administer antibiotics or other medications via the tube, this avoids repeated needles every time a treatment is needed.

Richard said he doesn't want to do physio today, he is too tired. He is also waiting for a CT scan (Computerised Tomography), to determine if a stroke has occurred during surgery and to see if this is any connection to the weakness occurring on his left side.

We had a long conversation about how things are, it helps if he can share how he's feeling. The frustration is immense, something he couldn't do in the beginning. He does have a friendly nurse on duty today who knows him well and this has made things easier for him. She told me that Richard is smiling right now and he looks more comfortable.

I spoke later in the afternoon to the same lovely nurse, she said she is going to ask the matron if it would be possible for me to visit.

During our conversation that evening, Richard had spoken to the Ward Manager, who had to get permission from a higher authority, to see if I could visit. He sounded tired. His PICC line had been fitted, but he now needed an X-ray to confirm if the line is positioned in the correct place. I was glad I had spoken to him as it appears he is having more one to one care, especially during the night.

Day 27

I didn't speak to Richard until the evening today. I wanted to let him get on with things as he was waiting for so many procedures to happen. He had a CT scan of his head and neck, I believe this was to check for any signs of a stroke. After this, he was told that the PICC line that had been fitted earlier, was not in correctly. This would need to be replaced, however, the team confirmed they would not be able to do this until tomorrow. He did say that his body felt like it had been run over by a bus, hardly surprising with all the checks and procedures going on.

The Super Ward Manager, as he is called, had come in to see Richard and to apologise for his first night spent on ward 304. He accepted that Richard had not been looked after in the way he should have been. Richard's only problem was he couldn't do anything for himself, but he is able to understand the tremendous strain that all the staff in the hospital were under.

Richard had an Echo (echocardiogram) of his left arm. His arm was still very swollen. The team were checking to see if there could be any other reason for this, apart from fluid retention. The results of the Echo confirmed that no blood clots had shown up and we felt that was more positive news.

He had an Echo of his heart, completed by a long-standing staff member, who knew Richard from day one, on his journey at the

QE. She was very happy with the way the donor heart was functioning. This was amazing to hear. It must be lovely for the staff to follow a patient who they have been looking after for so long, especially seeing them recovering from a transplant.

Richard had some physio, at the same time testing his reflexes and strength in his arms and legs. He will need to do daily exercises to strengthen all the muscle waste he has and to improve his strength generally. His arms and legs are still very swollen.

The staff remain concerned over the old driveline site, which still has puss in it. They have left the wound site open, to enable a slow healing process to take place. With the treatment they are using, this will hopefully reduce the infection.

It has been suggested that Richard needs at least 2000 calories intake a day. If he can do this with a normal diet, then the NG tube can be removed.

As a result of the steroid medication, Richard has developed Diabetes, which means he has become insulin dependent. This is another normal occurrence after a transplant of any kind, but one we hadn't been aware of, prior to the operation. In the long term, it is the hope that his sugar levels will return to normal function and he wouldn't need any medication at all.

Richard was chatty today and talked for almost an hour, always a good indicator as to how he's feeling.

He is still waiting for the results of his head scan.

I received a call in the evening, from the lovely staff nurse who had been looking after Richard earlier, to say I was able to visit tomorrow. She had most definitely pushed for us. It was the best news. I was so grateful, tears springing to my eyes, knowing at last, I was able to be with Richard, after all the weeks that had passed and everything he had been going through alone.

For a moment, I suddenly felt a tiny element of concern, over how we were going to react with each other, after such a long time apart and in such strange and unusual circumstances. How would Richard look? I didn't want to appear shocked or upset when I do see him, with everything that was going on, things I hadn't been able to see or share. Richard told me he had the same anticipation and a little anxiety about seeing me too. His arm was swollen and he was struggling to use it. His left leg was still not functioning or moving as it should and he was concerned about how I would feel seeing all these potential disabilities.

How silly we both were.

CHAPTER 15

At Last
The First Visit

Day 28

Richard called me early, to confirm I was allowed to come in today. What a long wait it had been, to be able to see my man at last. I was mindful that the whole country was in the same situation and each NHS trust had their own policies for visiting, but mask wearing was mandatory for them all. We discussed the best time to fit in around procedures that had been planned for his care that day. He said he had slept quite well but was still waiting for a new PICC line. They had to insert a canular for the time being, in his right arm, to take blood or administer medication and he was not finding it easy to move his arm.

After getting things together for Richard and traffic delays on the M6, I didn't arrive at the QE till 4pm, but sadly when I finally got there, he wasn't in his room. He had gone to have his PICC line re-sited and they had seen some fluid on his lungs, so they were going to drain it and test for infection. The nurse said he had gone down at 1.30pm, so he had been away for quite a while already.

I felt so disappointed that Richard wasn't in his room, no one introduced themselves or said hello, considering I hadn't seen Richard for 2 months, apart from the morning of his transplant and talking to him on FaceTime. Then I gave myself a good talking to. The staff on the ward were so busy with the extra Covid pressures, trying to manage and keep patients safe. I felt incredibly grateful that I was allowed to be at the hospital at all.

Just as I was feeling like that, the Ward Manager popped his head in. He wanted to apologise to Richard about the poor care he had received on Sunday night, after the move from CC and when he first arrived on the ward. He also asked me if I was okay and if I would like a cup of tea. I thought this was really kind and assured him I was okay and just incredibly happy to be here. I had brought my own flask of tea and refreshments, but thanked him anyway, most of all telling him how grateful I was, for allowing me to visit.

The PICC line team came in to say they hadn't been able to re-site the line and that Richard would have to go back tomorrow for them to try yet again. He did, however, have a drain put in to help ease the fluid that had built up in his right lung. This is another very common occurrence after a transplant.

Richard returned at 4.30pm, a bit fed up but generally quite bright.

We had our first emotional and extremely long hug. It had been the longest month of our lives, or certainly mine. I couldn't believe how good he looked, only seeing him on FaceTime previously, but realising he was tired from his long afternoon away from the ward. I think he's going to be okay though.

A little later we were joined by Guapo, one of the team of doctors who had also been looking after Richard for quite some time. We called him that name, which when translated into Spanish means, "good looking," he most definitely was, and he knew it. When we asked if he knew why we called him that name, he said he understood what it meant and he had been called it before. We found his response quite funny and a little cocky, but nevertheless a very good doctor.

He came in to fit another canular for the regular blood tests and antibiotics that Richard needed to have. Fortunately, Guapo managed to do this at the first attempt and Richard felt relieved that the prodding and poking for that day was over. Whilst the doctor was with us, we seized the opportunity to ask him about all the queries we had.

The chest drain had to stay in for around 48 hours, although there was very little fluid coming out. It is likely they would need to repeat a drain on the left side, as there was also fluid present there. We asked about Richard becoming a diabetic and if this would be a permanent thing. The doctor said it is always difficult to confirm, but most people who were not diabetic pre-transplant, will usually revert to normal levels, but it can take some time for everything to settle.

Richard's movement seemed better than I imagined, but I noticed he still has a lot of swelling on his legs and hands. He needs help to get comfortable and to move into a different position. I can see how extremely frustrating it all is for him and how little he can do for himself, but every day does seem to make a difference.

His NG tube had been removed today, so that will make him feel better and he can continue to eat normally. Since returning from theatre earlier, he had needed some oxygen, but this could be to do with the fluid build-up on his lungs.

All in all, it was a brilliant first day with my hubby, who has survived an operation against so many odds. To see him and just be able to help him in any little way I could, was the most amazing, rewarding feeling in the world. I think I have definitely worn him out, but in a good way. It was a moment when nothing else mattered, just me and Richard being together again.

ANOTHER AMAZING DAY

"Let's Get you Walking"

Day 29

When I called Richard today there was no answer, I presumed he had returned to theatre to have his PICC line re-sited. He called me back later and seemed quite upbeat and settled but had not yet had the PICC line done.

Physio had been in to get Richard standing. To do this, he told me he was in an incredible amount of pain in his legs, but he managed to achieve the task. It had taken exactly 4 weeks to make his first attempt to stand. At that moment, he said he felt like he might never be able to walk again. He did manage to stand though and that was a fantastic start.

The staff nurse, who had confirmed my visit, came in to say thank you to Richard for the goodies I had taken for the ward the day before. She had given Richard a kiss on the forehead for them. That's just the way she was, a caring and thoughtful nature, simply wonderful.

Day 30

Richard called me today, what a change from yesterday. He was in pain all over, mainly due to the fluid retention on his lung and the discomfort of the positioning of the drain, together with the activity of managing to stand yesterday.

It had been mentioned a couple of times that he had lost a small part of his left lung during surgery and I needed to ask about this. We have since learnt that this was due to the removal of the LVAD during surgery and the impact or damage that occurred to his lung. We always anticipated that the removal of the LVAD was going to be a long job, having been attached to Richard for the last 8 years.

He had also had the PICC line re-sited yesterday, so all in all he was feeling a bit battered and bruised.

Richard called later in the day to say Will and Yolanda, his brother and sister-in-law had spoken to him from Holland, they had also sent a lovely video clip. I kept asking Richard when he was ready to talk to his family. I didn't want to push or embarrass him before he was ready for this, physically or emotionally and even whether he was able to hold and operate his phone himself.

We chatted about things and discussed why he was so worried about money, as this had come up in several conversations. He said he kept thinking we had paid for private medical care and the heart transplant had failed. He thought it had all been a waste of money and the staff were coming with the bill to collect payment. He also said that there were a lot of private patients in ICU having cosmetic surgery, some of them were not happy with their procedures. I didn't think this could be true and none of it made sense, but when Richard was describing the situation, it must have all seemed very real to him.

Another thing he mentioned was we had taken the whole family away on holiday and paid for them all. Everything he relayed to me was about money. What's strange is we had actually done this, years earlier, to celebrate my 50th birthday. We had paid for 14 tickets, to take most of the family to Ibiza, only to miss the flight. I had got the wrong flight times, something I will never live down knowing my experience as ex cabin crew. Our friend, Carol, was waiting for us in Ibiza, she wouldn't believe we had missed our flights when we called to tell her. We managed, with the help of my very kind mum and dad, to rebook with a different airline for the next day. The story is never forgotten with the family. We should have taken off at 2.10pm, but somehow, I thought it was 4.10pm. The joke is, "What time is it mum, ten past 2?"

It now makes sense for me to understand what he had been talking about and the thoughts going through his mind when he couldn't communicate properly. Richard realises what he had been thinking during this period. This was largely due to the massive side effects of all the medications being given and the time he had spent in a coma. He talks more easily about things, with his thoughts getting clearer, which is comforting for me.

The worst thing he says is not being able to go to the toilet properly. He is so constipated and has taken all the laxatives he can, to get things moving, but things were still not happening.

The fluid still being drained from the right lung had now reached 500mls, this was a good sign and the doctor indicated this would be enough to consider the removal of the drain.

Day 31

The drain was removed last night, followed by an X-ray at 2am, to check if all was okay with the area. They have said they may need to repeat this procedure in his left lung. He was planned to go back today for the other drain, but an emergency came in. Someone had been stabbed and needed immediate medical attention. This gives a complete reality check as to what is happening in the background of this incredibly busy hospital and the sort of problems they are dealing with daily.

When we spoke later in the day, it was Richard who had managed to call me. He was now able to use his phone, without help from the nursing staff. Kris and the girls, our granddaughters, Poppy, Isabelle, and Evie were with me, it was nice that he got to speak to them all. We were in the garden, still trying to maintain distance and the girls were great at understanding and respecting the no hugs allowed rule. It was a good distraction, watching them as they played skipping, bat and ball or just running races. They always have great fun in the garden. It was so lovely for me to share in the joy and innocence on their faces, helping me to lighten my sometimes, thoughtful and sombre mood.

Richard was now managing to pick up and drink out of his cup with his right hand. Each day, with everything he has to contend with, such a little task like this can mean so much. It also shows how the body can slowly improve and recover and with patience and time, you can achieve anything.

We chatted for a while and agreed how lovely it would be once he is home.

Day 32

Today Richard had physio, he was able to sit out of bed in a normal chair with a cushion for 2 hours. The staff need to hoist him to and from the chair. This is a safe, but not easy, or very dignified way to transport a patient from one place to another, especially with a catheter still in. It is, however, essential to get a patient out of their bed. The physios say they are happy with the improvements that Richard is making.

He keeps adding things from his memory that are slowly coming back to him. He said he had seen or dreamt about his own funeral, which did throw me a little emotionally and again I wasn't sure what this meant. He said it was in our local church and he even mentioned hymns. Apparently, everyone was crying. This made me laugh when he said it. Had he had an out of body experience to remember this in such detail, or could it be a drug induced hallucination? The transplant team have said, this is not an unusual experience, for patients who have gone through the procedures that Richard had. There seems to be more and more of these thoughts coming out every day now. The most important thing is to just keep listening and talking about each experience as it happens, or as he can remember.

The doctors on the ward round have said they don't need to drain the left lung, instead they will monitor this, in the hope that things improve. The procedure to insert the drain for the left lung is more complicated and dangerous, the access for this is difficult, so they feel it is a safer option to monitor things.

In the words of the doctor that day, "Richard is doing fantastic."

Kate joined me for tea tonight, it was nice to have some company and we called her dad, to have a little chat. He was resting after the day spent in the chair. It must take it out of the body, with all the muscles that haven't been used for some time, but he said he was glad we had called.

Day 33

I didn't call Richard until later in the day. He was very tired and hadn't managed to get up today for the physios. They said this is normal and not to worry as it is easy to feel tired and overwhelmed. The physio team mentioned they could arrange a counsellor, to speak with him about his experience and to offer some support. Mental ability is just as hard to overcome as physical ability to. The medications Richard is taking can play a huge part in this.

Some transplant patients may need this counselling service. The service is offered due to the feelings that may occur for a transplant patient. This can relate to the acceptance of the donor heart and thoughts that can develop. The hallucinations experienced during and post coma, in some cases, may need to be de-coded. We agreed not to overthink things, to take one day at a time and Richard didn't feel he needed to talk to anyone for now.

I have pushed to visit again, to give Richard more mental and moral support. It's very difficult and extremely frustrating, listening to all that is going on and how up and down things are. I'm not able to help in any way. If I was there, I could take some much needed strain off the staff. I am the closest person to him, we should be on this journey of recovery together.

Day 34

I think someone must have been reading my thoughts, as thankfully, the Ward Manager has kindly agreed for me to visit tomorrow. Then weekly after that, to offer mental and physical support. It was the best news for me to hear and I breathed a sigh of relief. Having been Richard's carer for the last 9 years, I know he needed me in this capacity more than ever. I was still testing for Covid, twice weekly, in my own NHS role, so felt reassured by this.

Richard called later, to tell me he had managed to sit in the chair for 2 hours. He had also stood up twice and stood alone, with the help of a support frame. He said he feels better sat in the chair, this gives him a little more independence and makes him feel like he is on the way to normality.

The tissue viability team came in to look at the old LVAD wound. Whilst they are happy with how it is healing, his CRP infection marker was up to 80, so this needs monitoring. The team had told Richard that pre transplant, the infection on his driveline, had worked at least 2 inches further up the line. This would have been difficult for the transplant team to see and one of the main worries in treating and stopping the spread of the infection. Eventually, the infection would have reached the heart, this could have made it too late for an alternative course of treatment or transplant. I don't want to even think of the third option. All of this would have confirmed the team's worries and their justification for placing Richard on the urgent transplant list.

Richard has been urged to drink 4 protein drinks a day, 1 bottle contains 300 calories. This will help to build himself up for rehabilitation. He had lost a lot of muscle tone during the last few weeks.

One of the transplant team regulars, who has been a source of great friendship and communication during Richard's journey over the years, came in for a chat. He would always make us laugh, never taking anything too seriously. "Is the KLM man still here?" he would say. "Is he wearing his clogs today."

The transplant counsellor returned, to chat to Richard about his wellbeing. Richard agreed that he would ask for further help if he thought he needed it, but felt he was doing okay. It is reassuring to know, if a transplant patient experiences any difficulty with their mental health, there is someone available in a professional capacity to help talk things through.

Day 35 (Visit Day)

When I arrived, I found Richard quite bright. He had just been down to have his first biopsy, to check for any rejection of his donor heart. This is usually carried out every 2 weeks in the beginning. This increases to monthly then 6 monthly, as things begin to improve and the chance of rejection decreases. This could extend to yearly, or even longer if the patient has no other concerns or symptoms.

An Echo, X-ray and ECG are also carried out after this procedure. His familiar Echo technician carried this out at his bedside, as Richard wasn't able to get to her clinic room. She was extremely happy with the function of the heart. Her words were, "Looks incredible."

I met with the physio who will be looking after Richard. He told us Richard would need to rest after the biopsy for at least 2 to 4 hours, before he would be allowed to start any exercise. He asked the staff to get Richard ready, by positioning him in the chair. We discussed the lack of movement on his left side, with his foot and toes not working at all. He said sometimes there can be damage, it is unknown at this stage, how the use of this will return. There is a chance this could be permanent damage. He indicated his rehab was going to be a long road, but on a positive note, he said, it's quite possible that Richard could be up and walking in a couple of weeks.

I wasn't sure how I felt, when the physio began to explain about the damage to his left leg and foot. It never occurred to me that Richard may end up with more disability than he experienced before the transplant. His choices at the time had run out though. I knew Richard would find it difficult to accept the possibility of this. All he had gone through during the last few years and now reaching this final stage, we may need to be realistic about his recovery.

After we talked about it together, Richard said that he will have to work hard with the physio team to get himself walking again. We would both need to adapt to whatever we were faced with.

The OT team came to visit Richard and discuss exercises he can do when he is sitting in the chair.

Richard was hoisted onto the chair late afternoon. Witnessing this made me think how a patient must feel. They are completely at the mercy of the staff who carry out this procedure. It is also difficult to keep a patient's dignity intact. He described the process as necessary, but he couldn't wait until it was no longer needed and he would be able to move by himself.

During the afternoon, I got a large washing bowl, with lovely warm water in, to let Richard soak and wash his hands. I cut his nails, an impossible task to do yourself, with the dexterity he was struggling with.

Supper arrived, Richard stayed in his chair to eat, finding this much easier with a tray and a table.

The matron popped his head into the room, to see how things were going. I thanked him so much for allowing me to visit and the difference it will make for both of us. He said there was going to be an announcement soon, relating to visitors who haven't seen loved ones or a family member for over 2 weeks. I was reassured I would definitely fall into this category.

The transplant team called in to say, there had been no rejection at all from his new heart, in fact her words were, ZERO rejection. That was some much needed great news and extremely reassuring, with one less thing to have to think about. Richard may need a change or reduction to some of his meds now, the process after receiving this news. His meds are constantly being reviewed, to avoid any risk of rejection.

Richard was hoisted back into bed around 6.45pm, he had been able to sit out for a good couple of hours. He always looked glad to be back in bed. Although sitting out was giving him some much-needed exercise and independence, I could see how it was also mentally and physically draining on him, even just for short periods.

Day 36

I didn't speak to Richard until later in the day, it sounded like a lot had happened.

He had been taken for an X-ray, at 4am. This is commonplace as an inpatient, it's difficult to get seen during the day. It is also an essential procedure after his biopsy, to check that all is okay.

Due to the procedures in the night, Richard thought he was going to feel like rubbish all day. However, physio turned up to say, if he managed to get up, they would get him to the toilet and leave him to sit there for a while. There must have been some sort of negotiation between them. He was so desperate to sit on a toilet, instead of the indignity of using a bed pan. Richard managed to stand on to the frame (Sara Stedy), which I will explain about later. He was pushed into the bathroom and to the toilet. He said he sat for about 20 minutes, telling me he did the most enormous poo, which felt amazing. However, when he described it, he said that I couldn't possibly understand how difficult it was for him to do this

154

and the pain associated with it. I giggled to myself but didn't say anything at the time, thinking we would have this discussion later.

Having given birth to 4 children, I felt more than qualified in knowing the difficulty he may have encountered in trying to have a poo, however, this wasn't the time for competition. For Richard, it was a massive turning point. He felt it was his best achievement, after spending 36 days using a bed pan. From now on no more bed pans. After the relief of visiting the toilet, Richard sat out in the chair for a couple of hours.

He had his lower chest stitches removed and his dressing changed on the driveline site, this was a little sticky, but doing okay.

A doctor on the nightshift came in to say Richard would have to go down to theatre. They said a chest drain was needed, relating to the fluid that remained in his left lung. However, this never materialised. After discussing it the following day with the transplant team during their rounds, it was agreed there had been a little confusion around why this had been suggested.

Overall, another good day, but most importantly for Richard, he had been able to go to the toilet properly.

Day 37

I called Richard this morning and the nurses had arrived to give him a bed bath. He was very bright and chatty but told me to call back around 1pm, when all the morning team had done their checks. There is always a lot going on and the nursing staff are in and out of his room all the time.

When I called back in the afternoon, Richard was sitting in the chair. He was doing his planned exercises and looking very bright, cheeky, and above all, looking well.

His driveline site is still sticky and he told me that his infection markers are up again, CRP above 100.

Day 38

When I called Richard during the morning, he was already sitting in the chair much earlier than usual, this is a good sign. He must at last, be starting to feel a bit better to want to be up and in the chair.

He had called his brother, Hans, and sister-in-law Marjan in Holland. He wanted to update them with where he is, on his road to recovery. It was a great sign for him to make that call. He's not a man of many words when it comes to phone calls, but he can talk the hind legs off a donkey, on any other occasion. I took it as another positive sign that he had called his brother.

This was the only call I had today. I had a massive hedge cutting job on. We have an exceptionally long border laurel hedge, as our house sits on a corner plot at the end of the Close. We usually only cut this once a year, as it's such a massive job, but looks fantastic when it's finished. Jenny helped me and we managed to do the whole thing in a day, with a couple of tip runs in between. The neighbours often comment when they go past. "Oh, is it that time again," stopping to chat and catching up on how Richard is doing. It's become quite a thing when it's hedge cutting time and everyone says how great it looks once the job is finished. Every year, I say, "This is the last time, I'm not doing it again, it's too much," and I'm not able to move for 2 days afterwards, but I still do.

Day 39

I called Richard on FaceTime in the afternoon. He had asked the nurses to get him out of bed and in the chair. A plan of exercises had been given to him for his upper and lower body, some he can do in bed and some in the chair.

He had his chest supports out, these have been keeping the chest wall together and he was looking good. Richard said he felt like he no longer looked like Frankenstein. There are only 2 sites left now externally which need to heal, one being the ECMO site and the other the driveline site, both still require regular dressing changes. We discovered that the ECMO tube is the width of a hosepipe, so the hole in his groin was going to take a bit of healing to say the least.

He had sat for well over 2 hours in the chair, when the physio turned up later in the afternoon. Richard said it was too late to start doing anything, he was so tired by the end of the day. His legs still feel like lead weights and these appeared to be giving him the most problems.

Saying that, each time I saw him, his arms and hands seem to be getting stronger and I was noticing his dexterity was also improving daily.

I called Richard later, as Leo, our grandson was with me, so he had a little chat on FaceTime with his grandad.

Day 40

I called at 10.30am and Richard told me he was booked in with the physios at 11am. The physios realised that he needed to get going early to get the full benefits from the exercises. He had asked if they could take him to the toilet first, before going to the gym, it was obvious he was still using his negotiating skills to his advantage.

The doctor mentioned the left lung again, confirming they are not going to do anything at this point, as this would mean repeating quite a difficult procedure. They are hoping it will drain itself slowly. It was another small concern for us. We weren't sure about the implications, or extent of damage to the lung and what this could mean in the future. It did keep getting mentioned though.

The staff told me it was okay for me to visit again on Thursday, (Hooray). It feels like such a privilege, also something we both look forward to so much and the difference it was making.

Day 41

There is no physio today, I am sure Richard feels relieved about this. The thought of it must be overwhelming at times. They are, however, the only people to come and safely get a patient back on the move and an essential part of his recovery.

If there is no physio possible on a particular day, he always makes sure he does his own exercises. He stretches his limbs in bed or in the chair, or he tells me he will do them when he can't sleep at night. The physios have said they will bring some equipment to the room, to enable Richard to do further exercises in the chair. This is more relevant for his floppy left foot and toes, which are still quite concerning. He needs to concentrate on exercises for his feet and legs, to try and recover strength back, also to see if his toes will begin to move again.

The transplant team are with him, going through his green book and meds. He is currently on 21 different tablets daily. The green book is the same as the logbook, given to all patients who are fitted with an LVAD. It is also given and used after transplant. The vast number of medications, with times that patients need to take them, are written in the book. Patients must tick when they have taken each dose daily or they could easily become confused if this isn't monitored or logged.

Weight and temperature should also be monitored daily, this can be an indicator that things may not be well. Most importantly, alert a patient to the possible risks of infection or rejection of the donor heart. Whilst in hospital, the weight of a patient is recorded by using a weighing chair as soon as they are able to get out of bed.

Richard has meticulously managed his green book from the first day he received it, after being fitted with the LVAD. I sometimes joke about his slight OCD personality (Obsessive compulsive disorder), how he keeps everything organised, tidy and doesn't like any mess. I believe that it's this personality and positivity that has kept him steady and possibly even alive over the years, with no major events occurring. He has taken his meds religiously and on time, which has a massive bearing on the well-being of a patient. Richard continues to manage this with his transplant green book. The immunosuppressant drugs, are another vital part for the recovery and survival of all transplant patients, as forgetting to take these tablets could have a detrimental effect on their outcome.

His black bag from the LVAD days, was still on the scene, where he continued to keep his meds and paperwork. He didn't need this bag anymore, but continued to carry it with him, I knew he would find it difficult to part with it. He calls it his office. I am hoping eventually, when he is ready to let go of it, we will have moved on to a better place, but we have some way to go.

Day 42 (Visit Day)

During my drive to the hospital today, I got a call from our dentist. He had heard from his team at the surgery that Richard had received a transplant. It was a kind gesture. We chatted a little about how things were affecting everyone with the Covid pandemic. Everyone in their professional capacity was being affected, no one it seemed could escape it. All transplant patients must be registered with a dentist, in order to be accepted on the donor transplant list. Immunosuppressant medications can decrease a patient's ability to resist systemic infection. This reason alone is why good oral health is important.

Richard was already out of bed and in his chair when I arrived. The transplant team had also arrived, to teach him about the home medication and the green book again. We had ordered a new pill box with 5 and 7 day slots, to hold the many tablets and different times, needed to take his meds.

Richard was looking extremely tired today. He hadn't managed any physio and should have had a biopsy, however the doctor said it wasn't required for another 2 weeks. This was good timing given how he was feeling. We read this as a good sign that all was okay. If things were unsettled, this procedure would have been done.

After 3 hours Richard was back in bed. We managed to do a shave with the electric razor, he felt lovely, clean, and smelt wonderful, always wearing his favourite Hugo Boss aftershave.

I gave his feet a massage for relaxation, to try and stimulate his left foot and toes. I used my trusted Nivea Soft, that I never go anywhere without, such a brilliant moisturiser. I believe the whole family uses it, we could be a great advert for Nivea. Massage is one of the things the physios had suggested might help, it was certainly worth a try. His feet and legs are starting to move a little, but any improvement is slow, but better than no signs at all.

I sat and completed his green book for 1 week. It is still difficult for Richard to concentrate, write or complete even one page of his book. His shaky hands being another side effect from the medication.

All credit is given to anyone reading this who has had to recover and retrain their body after a stroke or accident, it must be the most difficult and frustrating feeling. Watching him manage to do the smallest of things, the time, concentration and effort required, was so humbling. We have no idea about the difficulties of living with any kind of disability and how we take for granted our health and ability to do things for ourselves. It made me pause for a moment.

By the time I left, he looked a little brighter and more cheerful.

Day 43

Richard had sat up today and managed to walk or shuffle as he describes it, 6 steps with his own support frame. He was back in the chair but had also managed the small exercise bike for 6 minutes, 3 minutes, without the motorised assistance. He did 3 minutes on the arm rowing machine. This is the same theory as the feet and legs, but instead it works for the arms. He was at last starting to see some progress, from pushing himself with his exercise and he felt better about achieving more movement. This made getting out of bed a little easier too. It was a great mental boost for him. He had to start believing that in time, things would slowly start to improve.

Physio told him they had ordered a left foot insert for his shoe, in the hope of giving it some support. It would also avoid the dragging that he was experiencing. It was still too early to know how his foot and leg would recover, if at all, but he was certainly trying with the exercises recommended for this.

Day 44

When I called early morning, Richard had just finished a good breakfast of Weetabix, yoghurt, and orange juice. It doesn't get more normal than that, he sounded like he was in a hotel, but I don't think he appreciated the joke when I said that.

He told me he was going to try and do his pill box, for one day at least. This would be good practise, to help him get used to all the different tablets and doses lined up in his side cupboard. The cupboard looks like a chemist's shop, there are so many tablets inside.

I called later and Richard had been in the chair for over 3 hours and was ready to get back in bed. He isn't being hoisted now, to make him move more on his own, but he still needs some assistance. By the time he was back in bed he was tired, but glad he had been able to get up and do something during his daily routine. He had managed to do his meds himself. It had taken him an hour to complete 1 day's tablets, but it did show that his dexterity was improving.

Another well-known consultant from the team, who had got to know Richard well over the years, popped in for a chat. He told Richard, however hard he might think his battle and journey is, he personally feels positive for a good recovery for him. What an extremely nice thing to hear. All these familiar faces of the team would pop in to chat to Richard on their rounds, or when they are covering the ward. During this time, they have all got to know him pretty well.

While the doctor was with him, he mentioned that not all GPs will cover the cost of some of the meds that Richard was on. For the time being, it is better to continue under the care of the QE, to ensure the responsibility, supply, and continuation of the correct medications.

Day 45

The same consultant popped in again today, to chat with Richard, as it was his weekend on call. It is so nice that Richard gets to see consultants, in a relaxed and friendly capacity. It's someone to bounce any questions to, should he feel concerned about anything. All the staff at the QE are so friendly, they feel like family, we cannot say this enough. Their informal, yet still professional manner, must have a positive effect on the recovery and well-being of a patient, particularly for Richard, who has been visiting the QE for the length of time he has.

Nik, Kelly, and Luca our grandson, had called Richard for a chat and a catch up this morning. They said he seemed very bright and he had been doing his daily meds.

Richard had spoken to the Ward Manager again, to ask about visiting. It was confirmed that I was okay to visit on Thursday.

Day 46

Richard had his catheter taken out this morning and is at last able to wee on his own.

Physio had been and he had managed to shuffle to the doorway, with some help. Although he said he was extremely tired after any exercise, it felt good to be able to do it, especially as he was now free of his catheter. He had sat in his chair and done the usual daily meds. When I spoke to him, he was much more fluent and chattier, another glimmer maybe of his former self, slowly returning. Little bits of progress every day.

Day 47

I received a text message this morning from Richard to ask for a new phone charger cable. He told me the old one isn't long enough and the text also read, **"I LOVE YOU xx."** It did make me smile and as I've already mentioned, Richard isn't the great romantic, but seems to know, when I may need a little pick me up. Even though I say he isn't romantic, there haven't been many days in our marriage, if any, that I haven't heard the words, "I love you." I expect our children may cringe reading this, but they do know we still act like when we were first together.

Richard is in my phone under ICE King Richard, the ICE standing for (In Case of Emergency). He is my contact person, we are all encouraged to have in our phones, should the emergency services ever need to contact a next of kin. King Richard is a joke I have with him, relating to his strength of character. He sometimes thinks and behaves like he is king of the castle and like any marriage, this has caused us several disagreements when we get annoyed with each other. However, this strength of character was something he certainly needed now.

He had done his meds but told me it had taken him over an hour to complete. Even though it's frustrating, it helps that he has a task to do every day. By evening he was tired again, from just walking small steps to the doorway with the physio team. He had got cramp, while he was walking and this had made things more difficult. The doctor is going to look at his statin medication, as

Richard's cholesterol was a little too high. One of the side effects from statins can be aches and cramps.

The physio team have said that tomorrow, they are taking Richard to the gym to walk the parallel bars, another huge step forward for recovery.

Day 48 (Visit Day)

I arrived about 1pm, the same time as the physio team turned up. Richard wasn't keen to do any exercise today, he said his legs were still heavy and painful, however, he agreed to walk down the corridor. I wanted to film it to show the children, but he said, "No don't do that." I felt embarrassed for not reading how he was feeling. Realising what a private person he is, he wouldn't want to fail this task, or be on film. I had only wanted to share some progress for the children, but at the same time acknowledging that he just wasn't ready.

With the support of a frame, he managed to pull himself up and walk down the corridor to the next bay, turn round and walk back. He then did 20 minutes on the exercise bike at resistance 1, which was a good start. When he is pushing on the bike, his weak left foot feels as strong as his right, but when he's in bed, or trying to move it on its own, it remains very weak.

We did his med box together. The new box we had ordered online had arrived, so we were able to complete his tablets for the next few days. I sorted through his clothes and got his socks, slippers, shorts, and t shirts ready for his physio session tomorrow and the coming days.

Day 49

This morning, an hour after Richard had taken his meds, he had a sudden drop in energy levels, which made him feel wiped out. The same tiredness seemed to be occuring each day. The meds all have an important role in his recovery but appear to wipe him out for quite some time. He knows however, he must get up as the physios will be arriving very soon.

I made him laugh when I told him Mitsy had pinched his socks, which were lying by the washing machine. She had put them in her bed in the kitchen. Mitsy has a thing about socks and if any are lying around, or near the washing machine, she always takes them and puts them in her bed. She doesn't chew, or make holes in them, but lays them next to her. It must be a comfort thing, but very cute. I'm sure she is missing Richard and knows something isn't quite right, she is most definitely looking after me.

I called the Patient Experience team, to check if they had found the letters I had sent to Richard earlier, just after his operation. The letters appeared to have got lost during the move between wards. The team were so helpful and said they had not managed to find the letters, but they were going to re-print them and deliver them to Richard that day.

By the time I spoke to Richard, it was early evening and he was back in bed. He said he had a great day in the gym. He had walked the parallel bars which he found liberating, he said it felt so good being able to manage this task. I wish I could have seen him but was thrilled anyway to hear that news. It was a huge leap forward for his mental wellbeing and independence. He had also worked on his arms and legs on the exercise machine.

He now has his walking frame left in the room. With the help of a nurse, he can get from the bed to the chair and also to the bathroom. The way his strength is improving, he will soon be able to do that alone. We agreed that if I am allowed to visit at the weekend, we would get Richard to have his first shower.

Richard is still on a high dose of Prednisolone, an important steroid medication needed after transplant, but these meds can cause shaky hands. His sugar levels are also still going up and down. The team have advised this will improve as the anti-rejection drugs are optimised.

The letters had arrived from the Experience team. He said reading them had made him feel very emotional. Previously, they had been read to him by the staff in ICU. At the time, he wasn't able to hold the letters himself, or even retain the information. Now he was able to hold them and read them word for word.

Overall, another extremely positive day.

CHAPTER 16

The First Shower

Day 50

After having a good day yesterday, how different Richard sounded this morning. Sometimes when I call him, not surprisingly, he is completely flat and today was one of those days. He is still experiencing the sudden drop in energy levels, shortly after he has taken his meds. This is making him too tired to even hold a conversation.

The weekends are always difficult as there are not as many staff coming in and out of his room. It can make a patient feel a little isolated, especially with no visitors. The physio team don't cover weekends either, so it is a much quieter time.

Hopefully tomorrow will be a better day, as thankfully I am allowed to visit.

Day 51 (Visit day)

I arrived earlier than usual, at 11.30am, traffic is always easier at the weekend. Richard still looked tired and very pale. I wasn't sure if we would get him in the shower, but he was up for it, so that was a good thing and we thought it would help make him feel better.

I got all the things prepared to go into the shower room, so we had everything to hand. We used the Sara Stedy, a brilliant piece of equipment consisting of a wheeled frame. You can push someone from A to B in safety, without too much effort for the caregiver, or the patient. For Richards mobility at this stage, it was perfect and a great tool to hold on to for safety.

I left him on the toilet for a while, another thing he could appreciate, when remembering his time spent with a catheter and bed pans. I helped Richard move from the toilet to the shower chair, then to the sink, where we were able to do a full shave and trim. We got the shower running and when the temperature was ready, I pushed Richard under the water, while he was still sitting in the chair. This was the first time he had not had to think about covering up drivelines or dealing with wires, before taking a shower and since the removal of the LVAD.

He just wanted to sit there, with the warm water running over him for ages. He described the feeling as truly liberating. He had spent 50 days with only a face or body wash, now he was free to shower, without any complications or equipment. Another positive turning point and I left him under the water for quite some time.

After drying off and putting on a clean T shirt and pyjama bottoms, the nurse came in to do his dressing on the ECMO site. There was still quite a big hole in his groin, from the ECMO tube, but the wound looked clean. I then moved Richard, using the Sara Stedy, back to his chair in the room.

Richard decided to call all the children by Facetime. He must have felt good to want to talk to all 4 of them. They are all quite different in their personalities and some of them certainly like to talk more than others, but that's what makes them all so special.

He had been so tired at the beginning of the day, yet here I was, seeing a new man, refreshed from his shower and shave, talking to all his children. I felt overwhelmed with emotion and gratitude, to witness how far we had come.

Staff came in to change his mattress, from an airbed to a normal mattress. This was to encourage and help Richard with his movement in bed. It is important he is able to move more easily, in order to avoid any bed sores. We finished the day by doing his meds together, some he had to re-order with the staff. The list of tablets he is taking is endless and he goes through his supplies quite quickly. The count has increased to 30 tablets per day.

In the evening, I left an exceptionally clean and refreshed hubby for my drive back home and whose positive description of the day had been overwhelming, including talking to all our children.

Day 52

Richard was looking very bright this morning, especially after yesterday's shower and shave. They had taken him to X-ray at 3am. The doctor confirmed with Richard that they are not going to drain the other side of his lung. He told him the fluid remains the same if not a little less.

He doesn't seem as tired this morning after his meds. Maybe his body is getting used to them, now everything is slowly starting to heal and his body is adjusting to the trauma it had been through.

Last night, he had walked with his frame from the bed to the chair and back. He hadn't needed any assistance from the staff. He said he had backache this morning, but this could be from the change of mattress. He had been able to sleep on his side and to move from side to side more easily, so the different mattress is working better for him.

Today Richard walked with the frame to the second bay along the corridor, sat down, then walked back to his room. The physio team have provided a shoe support for his left foot, which was still extremely dropped. This would still suggest that Richard may have suffered a stroke and it's important he lifts his foot more, to ensure he doesn't trip or catch the end of his toes.

One of the physio team, who had been working with Richard since he came to the ward, was going on holiday to Scotland. When he returned from his break, he was no longer allocated to Richard's ward. This was quite sad, as he had helped enormously in building up his confidence and getting him walking. Richard constantly asked the physio team, "How are you going to get me to walk again." The reply from the team was, "Give it time, it will happen."

Day 53

Richard was tired and sleepy this morning. Physio had come early to walk with him. He had managed to get to the 2nd bay and back, with his frame, but it had totally wiped him out.

The transplant team have said they need to have a talk with us both, regarding Richard's discharge from hospital. This would include how to manage things post-transplant, the discipline in life that is required, together with the management of his medication and return follow up appointments to the hospital. Another great sign, we were nearing that day and the word discharge had at last, been mentioned. At the same time, this gave us both a little concern, in the realisation that he still had a long way to go and was still needing a lot of support.

Day 54

Richard isn't feeling good today. The doctor has advised that a sample of urine should be tested, believing he may have another infection. It was confirmed later that he did have a water infection, so a course of antibiotics was started. He was feeling particularly rough. He couldn't manage to do physio, as he has a constant urge to pass urine and it was also painful when he did. By evening though, he had started to feel a little better, even after a small dose of antibiotics. The staff urged him to drink as much water as he could.

Richard has been told he is booked for another biopsy tomorrow.

The Ward Manager has confirmed that it is okay for me to visit again.

Day 55

When I arrived around midday, Richard looked wiped out. Physio had got him walking, but today, they had to go a different and longer route as there had been an emergency on the ward. The longer walk had been too much for him. The water infection was obviously not helping.

Guapo popped in to see Richard and to tell us that he was sadly leaving later that day. He asked us to complete a survey for him. The survey was about how we felt his care had been, over the period he had known and looked after Richard. It gave us another chance, to ask him all the questions that came into our heads, with the developments of the last 2 days.

The doctor discussed the infections that Richard seemed to keep developing, in addition to his water infection. He also told us that he had developed oral thrush, another common infection post-transplant.

It didn't end there either! They were going to treat him for CMV (Cytomegalovirus), another infection that can appear due to the body's low defences. He would need to start on another course of antibiotics for at least 3 to 6 months. We were both starting to feel overwhelmed, yet again, with the new set of hurdles that Richard faced. His CRP, infection markers, were also raised, to 103. No wonder he was feeling so poorly during the last couple of days, with now, 3 different types of infection floating round his body.

We started to wonder if there would ever be an end to all the infections that kept occurring.

One positive was that his urine output was better and not as painful since starting on the antibiotics, something at least, was going in the right direction.

There suddenly seemed an awful lot going on, with all these infections appearing in the space of 24 hours. Infections are a much greater risk for a patient, after any form of organ transplant.

On the journey back home that night, I began to sort the day out in my head and put things into boxes, prioritising the worry of each. I would always put some nice music on to help ease my journey home. I decided that it was negative energy and not helpful for either of us to dwell on things too much. I reminded myself just how grateful I am that he is still here and the excellent care he continues to receive at the QE. My final thought was that I was confident he will recover and he will be okay, everything was just going to take a little longer.

Day 56

Richard was brighter this morning, he had received his meds for the oral thrush, a liquid you have to squirt on the tongue.

We chatted about his physio session and did a little bit of home planning. We contemplated about how things might be when he eventually comes home. We both seemed to have accepted and moved on, from all the information and symptoms of the day before. What a difference a new day makes.

Day 57

When I called later today, Richard was aching from the walking he had done over the last 2 days and his chest felt very tight.

One of the regular nurses looking after Richard had given him a kiss on the cheek, when she had come in to see him. She said she loves looking after him. With her extremely vibrant personality, she always lights up a room with her presence and manages to put a smile on our faces. Thank goodness for those nurses.

Day 58

When I called today, Richard was watching the Grand Prix. This is the best distraction for him as he gets completely immersed in the race and the commentating. He was still aching from all the walking, but we agreed this was a good sign. His muscles were having to recharge, after an exceptionally long time of not being able to move any of them.

I asked Richard to check with the doctor about his results, regarding the CMV infection and what this means, in the long-term. He has had some extra bloods taken today. The doctor popped in later, to explain this. He said CMV can live dormant in most of the population, but raises itself, particularly when the body is vulnerable. Richard has been put on some more meds, to control and subside the infection and this will be monitored via his blood tests.

Richard repeated to the doctor, he thought the team at the QE were incredible and the doctor's reply in a comical way was, "Well how clever are we, that we have managed to fool you." What a great sense of humour they all had.

Day 59

I took Kate to pick Leo, our grandson up, from his other grandad, at Junction 14 of the M6. There were traffic problems as always, so we drove the scenic route, through Stafford and back to Crewe. The countryside is just lovely. It made me think I couldn't wait to get Richard home, so he is able to experience our beautiful surroundings and all that life has to offer us again.

Richard called when we were travelling home. He had an Echo after his biopsy earlier that day. The technician was happy with everything and said his heart was ticking along nicely. The results of the biopsy had recorded no rejection present, this means they can hope to reduce some more meds, which is always a good thing. Richard also had his ECMO dressing changed. He had missed the physio team today, due to all the other routine procedures that were taking place.

The Ward Manager had kindly agreed to my visit again.

Day 60

I called before I went to work this morning and all was good. We didn't speak again until around 7pm, after I had finished work. Richard had resumed his physio and had walked from his room at Bay 1 to Bay 24, which is a fair distance. The physio team now want him to try and walk without his frame if possible, this would be the next positive goal towards getting him home.

He had been for an X-ray, a routine procedure after a biopsy. He was transported in a wheelchair but was able to stand alone for this. Richard had already checked with the transplant team if they could reduce his meds, however, they said it wasn't possible just yet. (Quote, "It's a little too early after the procedures and before all the results have been read.")

Richard requested that I bring in some egg sandwiches on white bread, a favourite of his, when I visit tomorrow. It's the first time he has asked me to bring any food in, another good sign.

CHAPTER 17

Getting Ready for Home

Day 61 (Visit day)

I arrived about 1pm today, the doctors were with Richard. They are all keen to get him home and whilst medically he is ready to go, his mobility still needs to improve.

Physio arrived and Richard used crutches to walk to Bay 24 and back. He tried to use a step up, to exercise both his feet, but he wasn't able to do the step today. It is mostly balance and strength from his left leg and foot that are still troublesome. Physio showed him exercises that he can do at the bottom of the bed to help strengthen his legs, feet, and hips.

The dietician visited Richard to measure his hand grip. He achieved 29.5 on the right and 23.5 on the left. The average for men is usually around 40, so he still had a little way to go.

His driveline area was almost a third healed over and doing much better now. The Pico dressing seemed to be helping with this.

Later in the evening we got Richard in the shower again, after a change of clothes, he said he looked and felt like a new man.

I left the hospital around 8.30pm for my drive home and Richard looked happy and relaxed from our day spent together.

We are getting there.

Day 62

Richard had a good day when I called. He had been down to the gym and walked with one hand, holding onto the parallel bars. He had also been able to walk a small distance without support. This was an incredible step forward and I felt emotional listening to him telling me this, but sad also that I wasn't there to share in it. I was, however, able to feel the emotion and positivity of that moment. He had also managed to do some step-ups on the Reebok step with his crutches. Altogether, this had given him renewed confidence. He was starting to believe that it was possible to improve and recover, however long the process was going to take.

Richard told me there were a lot of other patients in the gym today, in a far worse position than he was. He said it had helped him to put things into perspective. Patients who are recovering from trauma and a long hospital stay can become self-absorbed with their own condition, thinking about it every minute of every day, so this was a good reflection.

Richard asked if he could try and climb the normal stairs, he knew this was another goal he had to reach before being discharged, but the physio team explained that he wasn't ready yet. He must try to build up more muscle tone before he will be able to attempt this task.

Later another comment made me smile about my not so romantic husband. Richard said he had thoughts about us getting married again, in the church in Cala Llonga and on the island where we first met. He said it had made him emotional thinking about it, always blaming any emotions on the medications he is currently taking. There is a certain amount of truth in this. Either way, it was a lovely romantic thought for the future and who knows what might happen?

Neil, a long-term work colleague, had called for a chat and to catch up with Richard. They had worked together for over 20 years. Neil had a fantastic sense of humour and they had always got on very well. It was another good sign that Richard was ready to chat a little more to friends and family.

Day 63

When Richard called this morning, he told me there was a chance he could be home the following week, but it's important that he is able to manage the stairs. His overall mobility is slowly improving and he is getting a little stronger. He wasn't sure if the physio team were coming this morning, so he managed to walk on his own with the support of his crutches, to the end of the corridor. This was a massive change and the first time that Richard had gone it alone and had the confidence to do so. The idea of home had obviously worked and made him push harder.

OT, (Occupational Therapy) had asked Richard if it was okay to contact me regarding his discharge, to discuss any arrangements we may need in place for him, once he is home.

Hans had called Richard to catch up with his brother and to send all their best wishes from everyone in Holland.

Day 64

The staff nurse in charge had told Richard it was okay for me to visit over the weekend.

Richard had walked to Bay 24 twice today, again under his own motivation and also completed 15 minutes on the cycle machine.

Willem had called from Holland, to see how things were going and to tell Richard he was fishing on the river. They would always joke with each other about the size of the fish they had caught, which of course, was always exaggerated. Sometimes on a visit to England, they were able to go fishing together, Richard had managed to get Willem into the local fishing club for the occasional stay that he may have with us.

Day 65 (Visit Day)

When I arrived today, the last 2 days had caught up with Richard and he was exhausted. I wasn't surprised, as this had been the first weekend when he had undertaken his own physio activity and he may have pushed himself a little too far.

We managed to walk together to Bay 24. Our lovely friendly staff nurse was on duty again and she reminded us that she would be coming to our wedding in Ibiza. I began to wonder what Richard had been talking about with all the staff, regarding this second proposal of marriage. He hadn't even asked me yet and he was obviously presuming I was going to say yes.

I thought it would be a good idea to take Richard downstairs, to get some fresh air and see outside. I persuaded him this would be a good idea, after checking with the staff, to confirm it was okay. We got a wheelchair and made our way out of the hospital. Bearing in mind he hadn't really seen proper daylight, only behind glass, or felt real fresh air for 64 days, a long time and not good for anyone's mental health. We sat on a bench outside for a while, just holding hands and spending a few quiet moments of reflection, with no words needed to be spoken. The warmth and love you can feel in that single moment is priceless. How lucky we were.

Whilst it was important to get Richard outside, I could see after a short time that he felt strange, a little uncomfortable and I began to think it wasn't such a good idea. He had suddenly lost the sense of security the hospital had given him all this time, another reality check of where we were and how slowly we needed to take things. I reminded myself that we must continue to take one day at a time.

When we got back to the room, Richard wanted to do some exercise and managed 30 minutes on the bike. In his mind, he knew he had to keep pushing himself, if he's ever going to get fit enough for home. I think our outside visit helped after all.

Day 66

OT called me today. They asked if I felt okay to have Richard home and to care for his needs where necessary. How could I not be? We discussed the home and any obstacles that could be difficult for him to manage. It was hard for me to imagine how the situation would be, until Richard was home. We are fortunate to have a downstairs toilet, so the only obstacle I could think of would be the stairs. All the relevant teams responsible for his care were working hard with him to overcome these problems before he left hospital.

Richard called later to say he had slowly managed to climb 9 stairs that morning, with help from the physio team, a huge hurdle ticked off now. He suddenly seemed to be moving forward at a faster pace both physically and mentally.

His diabetic meds had been changed to oral tablet form, yet another great sign. Richard would have to remain on these until further notice and monitor his own blood sugars at home. Hopefully, he won't need any treatment for this condition, as everything returns to normal levels. At last, everything seemed to be improving and moving forward for his discharge from hospital.

I told him I wouldn't come tomorrow, I suddenly felt incredibly tired. It wasn't surprising, given everything I was suddenly having to think about, including both the excitement and the anticipation for his discharge. Why are we so hard on ourselves during times like this, when your only choice is to keep going. However, things do have a way of catching up with you and your body tells you when it's time to stop. I'm sure it was mostly because I could see the discharge for home in sight and I had relaxed a little.

Day 67

The doctor had been this morning and is happy with the way things are going.

The driveline and PICO dressings had been changed, both were continuing to heal nicely. He was another step closer, to being finally free of all the different wound areas on his body, he has experienced over the years.

Richards legs were very tired and achy from walking the stairs and using the bike the day before. A good sign, showing that his muscles were coming back to life. We must keep hoping that those legs and feet can improve.

Day 68

When I called after work today, Richard was in bed as he felt shivery and his temperature had risen to 38.1. The team thought there was a possibility of a urine infection again, so antibiotics have been prescribed for 5 days.

The doctor explained that Richard can't go home just yet, not until they have managed the infection and reduced his temperature. They had taken the PICC line out to eliminate this, as a possible source of infection. Richard had been fitted with a canular in his arm, his pet hate, this usually catches on everything, but is essential to administer the antibiotics or take bloods.

The dietician had called to leave some leaflets and to discuss the importance of diet, in relation to keeping Richard's cholesterol reduced. Even though Richard has had a transplant, he still has to respect his hereditary condition of high cholesterol, this could mean a build up again in his arteries over time.

Richard went for an X-ray around 7pm, again standard procedure after a PICC line has been taken out.

Day 69

Richard is feeling much better today, the antibiotics must have kicked in. The doctor thinks the infection could be related to the old PICC line which has now been removed. He has already reduced his diabetic meds and steroids, a good sign that his body is settling a little more. A kidney and bladder scan have been booked, to check there are no growths or twists present. His CRP is 145, so still high enough to feel rotten.

The physios arrived for his daily exercise and Richard was able to do this today, even though yesterday, he had been feeling particularly rough.

I was told that it was okay for me to visit tomorrow.

Richard called me at 11pm, to let me know they were moving him to a Bay of 4 other patients. This unsettled him, given all he had been through and the importance of keeping him free of other risks. With Covid still around us, it was a huge concern for both of us, especially so close to discharge. This was due to a new patient being admitted, who needed a side room to await tests results and be in isolation. We will know more tomorrow, but Richard is unhappy, as well as annoyed that he has to move and the risks for him. It would also mean I wouldn't be able to visit tomorrow, due to the Covid risks for all the other patients in this Bay.

Day 70

Richard called me early as he had an unsettled night. He decided to use urine bottles, instead of using the shared bathroom. He was concerned about picking up anymore unwanted infections, that he was already having difficulty in managing.

The transplant team came to see him, but there was nothing they could do to move him. I noticed how quickly he became low in mood. He is trying to reason with how much hard work has gone into his care, then having it all compromised, by being too close to other patients with different medical issues.

Whilst I was talking to him, a patient from another room had come in to use the shower and Richard was moaning about the situation again. As the patient was leaving the bay, he turned and apologised for using the shower. He then explained that he was in a room with no shower, or washing facilities and that he was preparing to go for a lung transplant.

It really upset me and I felt concern for this person. I remembered, not so long ago, when we had to prepare Richard for his own surgery. I snapped, shouting at Richard on the phone and told him not to be so ungrateful and selfish. We had been in the same situation as this patient, who was alone with no support, due to the continuing Covid restrictions or even if he had any family at all.

I was glad to get off the phone and leave him with his own thoughts. Whilst I could understand why he was behaving that way, I didn't feel he was being fair. It was the first time I had got angry with him during his hospital stay, but I was annoyed at his insensitivity towards another patient. Being unwell for so long makes it difficult to see outside your own set of circumstances. My emotions were all over the place, feeling angry and sad that I had to shout at him. At the same time, I was crazily reassured Richard's fight for his own recovery, was still well and truly there.

I wasn't able to visit today, which was perhaps a good thing, given our previous conversation. It was better if we both had time to think about the situation that occurred yesterday.

Richard discovered that the other patient didn't go ahead with a lung transplant that day, but we are unsure of the reasons.

Day 71

I woke up this morning to a text from Richard, saying he had been moved to a side room, late in the night. He was obviously relieved and felt much happier. It also proves that he was right with his thoughts of staying protected, as they moved him to a side room as soon as they could.

He went on to have a more settled day, walking as far as he could, along the long horseshoe corridors and back. He would usually try to do this a couple of times in the day, to keep mobile and keep building his strength.

He had been told that his CRP is down to 40, so this has reduced quickly, but he's now being treated for E.Coli, another infection that has shown up in the tests. This was not what we wanted to hear, yet another infection.

He had been taken for a kidney scan but had no results back yet.

Day 72 (Visit day)

The doctor on examination had heard a rattle on Richard's chest and had sent him for an X-ray, to see if anything showed up.

Yesterday, we had decided to cancel my visit again until today. Richard seemed to have too many things going on the day before. I managed to arrive, after a longer than usual drive, at about 1pm. We hugged each other for a long time, especially after the words we had exchanged, two days before. We had a cup of tea, followed by our usual catch up. Although we had managed to have great communication over the phone, it's never the same as seeing each other face to face.

Whilst we were sitting chatting, both his brothers called, one after the other from Holland, which was lovely. They all had a long chat, catching up with how things were going. We joked that after the transplant, Richard might wake up and not be able to speak or remember the English or Dutch language. Listening to him speaking to his brothers, this most certainly wasn't the case.

Richard had another shower with my help. We decided to sort through his clothes, as "THE HOME" word had been mentioned a few times over the last few days.

The staff let Richard know that his CRP had dropped to 30. This was great to hear and meant that the antibiotics were working their magic.

He then completed his usual walk along the corridors. All the wards at the QE are on a horseshoe, so you can walk a full circle. It's the best way to get the exercise in, whilst staying close to help or assistance, if it was needed.

Day 73

Richard has been told the earliest he could be home would be Wednesday, or possibly Thursday.

He had gone for another walk with the physio, after falling earlier. Richard wanted to see if he was still okay walking, but with the support of physio watching over him. It was just bruising on his bottom, but his side was aching a little. He was able to continue walking okay, so little damage was done. The fall was due to his dropped left foot, which is still reacting more slowly and still difficult to move for him. Richard must always engage with this problem, before putting one foot in front of the other. This is not always easy and the split second he doesn't do this, he will run the risk of tripping or falling, which is what happened on this occasion.

Day 74

The transplant team have moved his home day to Friday. They have asked if I can come into the hospital, to listen and share the HOME from hospital chat on Thursday.

Richard's antibiotics have been increased again and he must take them for the next 10 days. He is still allowed to go home, even though they are continuing to treat him for infection.

He has done 2 walks today, being extremely cautious not to catch his left foot. He sounds much more positive, knowing that he is closer to going home and hearing the words we have all been waiting for.

Day 75

Richard didn't sleep too well last night, but I expect there are lots of things going through his mind. He is anxious about getting home, thinking about how he will cope with the changes, both mentally and physically. He is still waiting for his blood results, to see the reason for this new 10-day course of antibiotics. The staff have said it is more likely to be precautionary, after the infections of the last week. The doctor explained that one of our friends from the transplant team will be coming in tomorrow, to complete the discharge chat.

Richard has been pushing himself more today, going on the exercise bike and walking his usual route around the corridors.

I got a call from Florence today, a long-time family friend, who wanted to catch up with me and to see how things were going. My parents had holidayed with Geoff and Florence so many times over the years. They are one of those couples, who don't seem to age. It was really kind of her to call and since losing my own mum, she has been a great listening ear, for all I have had to share. It came at a time when I most needed it. I was very tearful after the call, thinking of my own mum and how much I missed her.

Day 76

When I arrived today, we had our usual catch up about how everything was going. We got into the habit of calling these moments, our business meetings. This was to make things a little more lighthearted, given everything that was happening daily and how organised we needed to be.

One of the transplant team joined us to do THE HOME discharge chat. They spent a long time going through the necessary and important facts of leaving hospital, along with the care needed to protect yourself after having a transplant. They also informed Richard that he is no longer able to eat some of his favourite foods. These consist of mussels, prawns, and any other crustacean. He was told to look at the foods, a pregnant mum is advised not to eat and follow the same guidelines. One of Richard's favourite foods was mussels, but unfortunately these were definitely off the list now. A small price to pay though.

A transplant information book was given to him. The book includes everything a patient needs to know, from the start of the process, being accepted on the waiting list, to the operation and recovery afterwards. It also includes and explains the medications a recipient may need to take, including the possible side effects that can occur from each of them. It offers contact information, should there be any personal issues experienced post-transplant.

We were also made aware of the importance of taking extra care in the sun, ensuring the head is covered and always applying a factor 50 sun cream. The medications that are required to be taken for the rest of your life (immunosuppressants), can increase the risk of skin cancer, especially if a person is exposed to the sun for long periods of time, or if they get sunburnt.

We discussed the donor heart, which the team will only talk about if they feel you are ready to, or you have asked about it yourself. You can find out the age and sex of the donor, but no personal details are disclosed about the donor, or the recipient, either way. We both chose to hear this information, but did find it incredibly difficult and humbling, after we had been told. All you can think about over the next few hours, days, weeks, probably forever, is the donor who had lost their life, in whatever sad way it was. You also think of the family, who during their grief, were able to make the selfless decision, to allow the process of organ donation to take place. It makes it all very real and thought provoking and possibly one reason why the team don't discuss this too soon after transplant.

Richard was quieter than normal today and his stomach was a little queasy. I put it down to nerves and anticipation of leaving the hospital with his incredible support team around him. Or it may have been talking about the donor, as it's impossible for the information not to affect you in some way.

We both felt better though, after our HOME discharge chat. It was a lot of information we had to absorb before leaving hospital, but important to help Richard stay safe and disciplined. It was nice to have one of the familiar faces from the transplant team talking to us, it also helped us when he delivered the information about the donor heart.

I was driving home later, reflecting on the information we had been given that afternoon. It had been a particularly long day.. I was overcome with emotion thinking about the details we had been allowed to share about the donor heart. It was the only thing I could think about.

I called Richard, as I needed to share this whilst it was so raw. He said he was feeling the same. We both agreed, at that moment, to keep the information between the two of us. We didn't feel it was appropriate to share the donor's information with anyone else and felt it would be disrespectful. We will always be eternally grateful to the donor and the donor's family, who so generously and selflessly gave Richard the chance of continued life. I am not sure how other transplant patients manage this information, but we felt we had made the right decision for us.

From the information I have gained by asking professionals about this experience, it appears that some, if not most recipients, sometimes find it hard to accept that they have received a donor organ.

We both felt relief and agreed it was a conversation we needed to have with each other. After saying goodbye to Richard, I carried on with my own thoughts, during the rest of my journey home. I said a prayer through my tears for the donor's family and hoped they would be able to find peace in time.

I was just nearing home, driving my last few miles. The moon was full and looked so beautiful in the clear skies above. Just as I was thinking how lovely it all was, the most amazing shooting star, swept across the sky. It completely took my breath away. Whatever I wanted this to mean, I wasn't sure, but it did make me shed a few more tears, for whoever my tears were for.

(HOME AT LAST)

Day 77

I made a bit more of an effort getting ready today, almost like I was going to a party. Strange really, but inside I wanted to look the best I could.

I arrived at the hospital about 2pm. Richard's discharge letter had already been completed and he was now waiting for his meds to be delivered.

I had taken some gifts and a card for the staff. It wasn't nearly enough after all they had done to look after Richard. I decided as soon as I could, I would do something to raise some funds for the transplant team, in the hope of being able to give something back. How do you say thank you, after all this time and for all the care.

We waited for one of the nurses, who would take us down to the car. It was quite a way to go from the ward. As we left, a few of the well-known staff clapped Richard out, it was lovely and a little overwhelming. As we know, there had been a lot of other people suffering and recovering from Covid and this was a familiar site around many other hospitals. I joked with the staff and said they must all be relieved and glad to finally get rid of him, but also more importantly, the feeling was, he has made it. Richard was coming home, it was an absolute miracle.

He didn't show any emotion, but there was a lot going on and I knew his mission was to get out of the hospital and he had to put all his concentration into that moment. In total he had been an inpatient at the QE, for over three and a half months. To witness how happy he was, when he reached the familiar sight of our car, was enough. The staff helped us with all his things, and we had a couple of hugs before we left. It was impossible not to.

The journey home was going to be a long one, as it was Friday afternoon on the M6, but none of that mattered. We had done the same trip so many times. The most important thing was leaving the hospital together, at last, ready for the next chapter of our life.

When we arrived home, Jenny had put some red heart balloons outside the front door and laid some flowers and hearts on the table in the lounge. It looked lovely and I appreciated the effort she had made. Kate popped in, as soon as she knew we were home, straight away wanting to hug her dad. It made me cry, realising that all our children and grandchildren would need and want to give him a hug. This would carry so much risk and we did have to be incredibly careful, with Covid still present in our everyday lives.

I had bought a Chinese meal from Marks and Spencer. Richard had one cold Corona beer and I had a glass of wine, our own small celebration for him being home. He had waited a long time for this moment.

The heating was on, the candles lit and we both just sat together, quietly contemplating, feeling truly blessed.

WE WERE HOME TOGETHER

CHAPTER 18

Reflections on Recovery

A fter arriving home, my biggest concern was that Richard wasn't going to be the same since his transplant. How that might affect our relationship, in which we have always been open and honest. My mind was in overdrive and I couldn't get this thought to go away. Although I knew Richard was elated to be home, at the same time he was feeling a huge level of apprehension without his nursing team around him.

The transplant team had repeated many times how long his recovery could be. He laughed though, saying he is lucky to at least have his number 1 nurse (me), on hand, 24/7. Most of all we could have the biggest and longest hug, without the batteries from the LVAD digging into each other's sides, something we hadn't be able to do properly, for such a long time.

The first day we were home it rained all day. Neither of us bothered to get dressed and decided to have a pyjama day. It felt right, warm, and cosy back in our home together. There was nowhere to go out to, the risks of Covid were still high and Richard needed some time to settle. We did speak to all the family on FaceTime, to let them know that dad was home and doing okay.

We managed to sort through all Richard's meds, put them in order and went through his old LVAD equipment that he no longer needed. We will ask the hospital, at the next appointment, what we should do with it all. In a small way, it would be difficult to part with it, still not believing that he didn't need it anymore, but it was true, he didn't.

By the second day, Richard managed to have a shower, using a chair we still had from when my mum's own mobility had become difficult. It was a life saver, as the floor was too slippery to stand, with his unsteady feet. Why hadn't I thought about this problem earlier? We later fitted a handrail, onto the wall and inside the shower cubicle, so he was able to pull himself up, or simply hold on.

In the first couple of weeks of Richard being home, it was a very strange time for us both and we knew we might need a little bit of adjustment. Whilst we were relieved and happy to be back together, Richard struggled with his own difficulties. He was trying to get his body to work again, with the new challenges and obstacles he faced in his home surroundings.

He was still experiencing the same problem, after taking his meds. His energy levels would drop and he needed to rest or sit down for a while. We hoped this would improve, but it was still impacting his ability in the mornings. However much the hospital tries to prepare you for home and the challenges that may lie ahead, there are still so many physical and psychological changes that need to be overcome.

I too, was also trying to adapt to the change of circumstances, now Richard was free of the LVAD. I could never have anticipated the enormity of the emotions we were about to face. We certainly had a reality check, one the transplant team had spoken to us about, explaining that having a transplant is not always a quick fix.

Richard seemed far away at times, even more so since he had arrived home. I found that I suddenly felt uneasy and nervous around him. I wasn't sure how to be or look after him in my role as carer, which had now changed. Whilst he still needed me, it was no longer in the same way as before his transplant. This was a new situation I had to adapt to. I felt like I was treading on eggshells, in order not to fuss him too much, but at the same time, trying to help him when he needed it. I couldn't work out how I fitted into this new scenario, or what my role was. I tried to hide how I felt, or so I thought. Not being with him each day, since his transplant, meant I hadn't witnessed or moved along with his slow recovery, or to share in that process. This made it more difficult to assess his care needs.

The most difficult task for him was trying to get out of bed in the morning. It was quite an ordeal, a strange experience, putting your feet and legs down on the floor and yet feeling they don't belong to you. His confidence had dropped too, even though he was home and in familiar surroundings. He described his legs as tingling and painful, like lead weights, just like he had explained, when he was in hospital. Each morning, he was never sure that he would be able to stand at all, saying he felt that his legs could just give way. Coming home feels like a huge setback for him.

I asked Richard how this was making him feel in the early days of his discharge from hospital, to try and understand what was going on in his head about his recovery. He said, as a positive person, he was always hoping that his mobility would improve, but there was a level of acceptance that told him this may be as good as it gets. He knew things would take time for him to adapt to any changes but was still thankful he had made it this far.

The transition from hospital to home would take time to adjust, after everything he had gone through, I needed to keep reminding myself of that. It was important I remained extremely patient and didn't try to rush things, or even hope for a recovery that may not be possible. When I think back, to just before the transplant and afterwards, I am not even sure what my expectations were if any, only that I wanted my Dutch DJ to live.

I needed to calm down a little. Although I had learnt how to counsel myself over many things, I do believe the carer role is a difficult one. Sometimes that person can be forgotten, in the day to day journey of surviving emotionally and looking after someone. In saying this, I would hate for the sympathy card to come my way. Even through everything, I was able to carry on with my life, go to work as normal, which had in fact, kept me sane, strong and was a great distraction.

A few weeks passed and this subject came up in conversation. Richard indicated that he felt I was disappointed with the outcome of the transplant. I must have made him feel that way, by constantly searching for other ways to improve his mobility. It was probably too soon to consider this. I was researching exercise, swimming, and physio, in the early stages of him being home, but in Richard's words, he felt like I was being a pushy woman. I was always looking for another way, to try and improve the movement of his legs and feet, but most of all, his pain. It was like I was on some kind of recovery mission for him, however, it would appear this came across as a little controlling. Richard says he needed more time to take things slowly, while sorting out his own mind and body. Also, since coming home, the feelings, dreams and memories of ICU were constantly returning to his mind and he was trying to make sense of them all. Initially he said it was all a bit too much.

I apologized for making him feel that way, this had obviously not been my intention. I was looking to find other treatments, in the hope this might improve his quality of life and ultimately help him feel better. In reality, why had I been trying to do this? Nearly all these kinds of services relating to his recovery were not available. With Covid, things were still far from normal. It made me think a small part of me was frustrated. Richard hadn't come home ready to run a marathon and perhaps subconsciously, I was even a little disappointed, like he said. It was important we talked this over and he said he could understand why I was pursuing those avenues. One of the things Richard reminded me of during these discussions, was when he told the nursing team that everyone needs a Shirley in their corner. That made me feel somewhat reassured about being a pushy wife earlier and that some of it was perhaps needed.

12 Month Calendar

During the first few weeks and months after the transplant, Richard was monitored on a regular basis. The hospital issues a 12-month calendar of dates for check-ups, that you need to attend. The first outpatient appointment was only 2 days after his discharge from hospital, when we had to return to the QE. Richard did manage to walk slowly from the car park up to the hospital. I collected a wheelchair from the reception area, to make things easier, he was still getting extremely tired, doing the smallest thing.

Whilst he was having his biopsy, one of the transplant team came to chat with me, which was lovely. He asked how I felt Richard was doing. I explained how we had both been feeling and he could understand all of it. He said Richard would need to start believing that he is well now, both physically and mentally, but his overall recovery will take some time.

I had my laptop out and we joked about my book writing. I told him I would like to share the journey that Richard had been on, including the diary I had kept, during his time in hospital and since his transplant. He said maybe I could get it put into a movie. It made us both laugh, discussing who would be best to play the parts of Richard and myself.

After Richard's checks, we met up with his regular cardiology consultant, who has known Richard from the beginning. Whilst his consultant remains professional, the appointments are always extremely relaxed and informal. We are able to discuss anything with him. I'm sure he thought it was pretty incredible, seeing Richard walk through his door, especially no longer wearing his LVAD. He discussed how poorly Richard had been, reminding us of their A to Z plan. He confirmed how the plan covered every eventuality they could think of, that may occur during surgery, or after. We all agreed, it must have worked. The doctors were all amazed that Richard had made it through, confirming his recovery had been slow and would continue to be so.

We discussed the dreams and hallucinations that Richard had experienced and which he was trying to come to terms with. During one hallucination, he thought he was having his transplant operation in India, at a cost of £38,000. We had sold some land, (I don't know what land), to pay for this. Such crazy thoughts that felt so real at the time. He also mentioned the city of Mumbai in India, as well as the exact cost of the operation. This may connect with our first conversation we had together, when he had just come out of his coma and he asked me if I had got everything in order.

Another recollection was being fearful of the meds or drugs, he was being given. Apparently, I was fighting the staff, to stop them from administering these drugs. Richard had said, "Get that bottle in the corner and clock her one." I presume he meant the staff member, who he was trying to stop.

We were assured by the consultant that it was normal for all these dreams to appear in the memory, after transplant. The medications Richard had needed, would take quite some time to work through his system and could be one of the reasons this happens. This was a great first check-up appointment, back at the QE, with all our questions answered with care, but most of all, concern for the well-being of Richard.

It was at this point, I stopped writing my daily diary. I'm not sure why, but I must have felt we were on the right path and Richard was back home with me now.

CHAPTER 19

Infection Again

Over the first few months after leaving hospital, Richard yet again, struggled with a constant urine infection. He was referred to the Urology department at our local hospital, to investigate if any underlying causes were present. Fortunately, nothing significant was identified. The consultant, at the QE, indicated the infection was more than likely due to the length of time he had needed a catheter, after the transplant operation. Once again, it felt like Richard was never going to be free from infection. As one infection settled, another one seemed to appear. After several months and long courses of antibiotics, his infection did subside for a while.

However, in May 2021, 10 months after his operation, Richard had felt quite unwell over the weekend and his temperature was raised. After speaking to the transplant team on the previous Friday, they wanted to find out what was happening with his meds. Richard had changed to a new immunosuppressant drug the week before. This was due to his kidneys becoming compromised on a previous medication. We thought this may be the reason for him feeling so poorly. Sometimes these symptoms can be a sign of rejection of the donor heart. Signs of rejection are the same as for heart failure, flu-like symptoms, tiredness, breathlessness, and swollen ankles. We also couldn't be sure if the same urine infection had returned, but Richard didn't feel his symptoms were the same.

The team at the QE wanted Richard to go to A and E at our local hospital. As he was feeling so unwell, he didn't want to sit there for hours, particularly as the Covid risks still remained. We knew after speaking to our GP, also on the Friday, there was a huge waiting time at A and E, both in our local hospital and over at the Royal Stoke. We agreed with the QE and our GP to monitor the situation on an hourly basis and would ring for an ambulance, if things changed, or got worse. Richard was booked for a routine blood test at the QE, the following Monday, he wanted to try and hold out until then. He managed to struggle through the weekend with bed rest and paracetamols, arriving at the QE for his blood tests early Monday morning. I dropped Richard at the front of the hospital, then went to park the car. I collected a wheelchair from the reception, as by this time, he was feeling quite lightheaded.

After his checks had been completed, we settled in for a possible long wait for the results. As a routine, I had come armed with a flask of coffee, tea, and snacks. I always brought my trusted laptop, which I seemed to carry with me everywhere and I was able to continue writing his story. We found some comfy seats and just settled in to wait. It's amazing how time passes sitting in the outpatient area, people watching and seeing the hustle and bustle of the very busy hospital. It also gave me another chance to reflect on things, sitting in the reception area of this vast hospital. Richard had got his coat round him and tried to sleep in a chair as we had no idea how long our wait would be.

The team didn't call until 4pm when they said they wanted to admit Richard, as things were a little out of sync, as they described it. His infection markers, CRP were high, at 200, which meant he was more than likely suffering from Sepsis. They didn't have a bed, so suggested we go home and wait for a call to come back in. We didn't feel this was a great prospect. However, whilst Richard was talking to them on the phone, a bed became available and he was able to be admitted. We had brought a few things with us, just for this eventuality.

We made our way to the ward and were thankful that we still had the wheelchair. The corridors at the QE seem to be miles long, keeping the wheelchair was a good idea. What a sense of relief for both of us that Richard was admitted, along with the level of reassurance we always felt, when he was back in the hands of the brilliant staff at the QE. We hoped they would be able to stabilise his condition and get him back on the right track.

Richard's stay in hospital, was just over a week, the antibiotics had worked their magic and he was feeling much better. His meds had been regulated, this seemed to help with his overall well-being. The hospital was under pressure to release beds, due to the Covid pandemic still requiring many admissions. Richard was more than happy to be discharged and he was able to continue with his antibiotics at home.

A few days later, his blood tests were repeated at our local hospital. This was to check on his kidney function and infection. The GP called the same day, late in the afternoon, to say he wanted Richard to go straight to hospital. His kidney function results were raised, as well as his CRP. We called the QE team for advice, after asking the GP for the levels of each of these results. Whilst the team understood the GP's concern, the results were in line with a transplant patient. We called the GP back to explain this and thanked him for his concern. As we had another appointment with the QE the same week, they were happy for us to wait to attend for repeat bloods, as long as Richard was feeling okay. They told Richard to bring a few things with him in case they wanted to admit him again. As it happened, all was okay and he didn't need to be readmitted.

Just when we thought we were out of the woods for infection, his feet and legs started to cause more discomfort than usual. This time he had swelling and redness on his right leg. It was quite painful and red and we knew this can be an indicator of thrombosis.

Richard spoke to his GP first, we were fortunate he was on duty, to explain his symptoms and he was asked to come to the surgery straight away. His GP reassured us and ruled out thrombosis after doing some tests. He did think it could be a condition called Cellulitis, which needs monitoring and Richard was given yet another course of antibiotics. The immunosuppressant drugs, which are vital after transplant, are reducing his antibodies and therefore compromising his ability to cope with infection.

A Year Later
June 2021

A year after transplant, things were still very up and down. This morning however, when we were having a cup of tea together, Richard said that his big toe was responding slightly and he was able to move it a little more than before. It was his birthday and it had been almost a year since his transplant. Although only a small sign, there couldn't have been a greater gift at that moment. It shows the length of time the body needs to recover in the smallest of ways, the small exercises he had been doing, had paid off.

I had spoken to a physio at our local hospital, and she explained this in more detail. She said that sometimes after trauma or injury, any nerve damage can take a long time to recover. How true had that statement been. It had been a year for his foot and toes to show some signs of recovery and movement, incredible really and proves how clever the body is. Our GP also commented on this, saying the brain prioritises the order of need for survival. In Richard's case, some other organs and certainly his legs, were not a priority during this time.

Richard had stumbled and fallen a few times over the last year. This was always a fresh reminder at how much he had to concentrate when he was walking. We ordered a splint online to insert into his shoe, to try and keep his foot straight and to correct the drop foot. This had limited success as it was extremely uncomfortable to wear. He did manage to find an alternative online. This consisted of a strap put around the leg, with a cord that fastened onto your shoelace. This kept the foot at 90 degrees and stopped you from falling on your face. It was also much more comfortable to wear.

Using the stairs before transplant was not easy and still remains difficult. Richard leans against the wall with his left side and uses the banister rail when he is going down, in a sort of sliding action to avoid falling. When he goes up the stairs, he uses the banister to both support and slowly pull himself up.

The transplant team listened to Richard explaining about his feet and legs during one of his check-ups. Their reply was, providing the blood flow to his legs is okay and this had been checked by the consultant, they don't have any real concerns. They discussed other reasons that may cause this discomfort, such as nerve damage, circulation, or age-related issues. If this problem continues, they suggested Richard refer back to his GP to investigate further.

We followed the appointment calendar issued by the QE after transplant and to complete each of the checks needed during the first year. These started off fortnightly, becoming less frequent as the months went by, apart from the occasions when his infection markers made him unwell, requiring our extra visits. In all this time and after having biopsies on a regular basis, he has not experienced any rejection at all from his donor heart. This itself is truly remarkable and we believe it to be from a combination of things. A good donor match, excellent management of the medications by the transplant team, to reduce the risk of rejection, alongside Richard's discipline for taking them on time and maybe, a little bit of good luck.

After each visit that included a biopsy, the team would analyse the blood results. Between 5pm and 6pm, the team would call with the results of any potential rejection and any increase or reduction in medication was confirmed the next day. At 12 months, the team write on your calendar MOT due. We found this quite funny, being compared to a car's maintenance but happy that it was a significant milestone to celebrate.

By August 2021, we were out buying trainers for Richard to start back at the Cardiac rehab gym, things were slowly starting to re-open after Covid. He was still extremely slow in movement and easily getting tired. We were hoping that attending the gym would help his energy levels and general wellbeing.

He contacted the Royal Stoke Cardiac rehab team, where earlier the classes had been stopped due to Covid. At the time of the call, they didn't have any spaces, but within a couple of weeks, a place became available. His first session was at the end of August. Richard found the sessions at the gym a positive experience and an additional benefit that he was able to get out of the house.

CHAPTER 20

Emotions

The first time we went out socially since transplant, was to visit friends in their garden, for a BBQ. The Covid restrictions relating to this had been lifted and it was so nice to be able to share these moments again. We spent a great evening, just like old times and enjoyed what seemed like the simplest of pleasures.

The following day, we watched the Dutch Grand prix, with the huge amount of spectators covering the grandstands, dressed in their patriotic colour of orange. It was a brilliant site to see. Richard without any doubt, is a huge Max Verstappen supporter and enjoys great banter with one of our grandchildren Kristian, or KJ as we call him. KJ is a fanatic Lewis Hamilton fan, so every race they continue their great rivalry. When the Dutch National anthem was performed before and after the race, we were both close to tears, with Richard especially proud of his Dutch heritage. We laughed at ourselves for getting emotional but understood the reasons why. Richard, as always, blamed it on his medications.

For a long time, I found I hadn't been able to cry easily, feeling completely emotionless, like everything I might or could feel, was locked away, something I cannot explain. Since Richard's transplant, I've noticed, the tears have slowly started to flow again and especially, since writing this book. It has helped us both talk openly about the chapters in our lives, how each moment has affected us in different ways, or even in the same way.

The biggest and only disappointment for Richard since his transplant is the pain he still experiences in his feet and legs. They continue to give him discomfort on a daily basis. The difficulty it took the team to remove the LVAD, and length of surgery has possibly contributed to this. He hopes there is still room for improvement and does remind himself constantly how far he has come, reflecting on his many years of illness. He is now, however, able to look forward to life again with his family, including his walks with Mitsy. The cloud of uncertainty that had been hanging over us for so many years, was at last, slowly starting to lift. There isn't a day goes by when I don't pinch myself to acknowledge that thought.

In the beginning of his recovery, if Richard did feel a little low or frustrated with the slow pace of his improvements, he would watch a programme called "Heart Transplant" (A Chance to Live). It's a documentary, filmed at the Freeman Hospital in Newcastle upon Tyne and follows 7 patients over a year, who need a heart transplant. Richard says it balances things out watching this. It makes him appreciate being alive, surviving it all, from the teams looking after him, but especially remembering the family of the doner organ.

Another moment, a news item, told the story of a man aged 91, who had a heart transplant 31 years ago. We watched this in awe. Everyone is different, but we believe the average expectation of heart transplant survival is about 12-14 years. Listening to this story was reassuring and I am sure gives hope to many. I joked with Richard, I was never going to get rid of him at this rate, the banter we can have with each other.

(Ibiza) again
June 2022

It took us quite some time since his transplant, before Richard was able or well enough, to travel back to Ibiza. Our spiritual home, where it all began and quite a different experience, now Richard was free of his LVAD. We continued in the same way as before transplant, allowing ourselves plenty of time to get through check in and security, walking slowly, at our own pace and to ensure we minimize any stress.

We met up with our old friends, who we had only seen once over the past couple of years, due to the Covid restrictions and Richard's timely transplant. Gill and Charlie had always been a great listening ear for me whilst Richard was in hospital, were able to fly out for a couple of days to join us. They said it was on their bucket list to eat out in Ibiza with us. We ate at our favourite restaurants, which are "Cas Pages" near San Carlos and "The Wild Asparagus" in Cala Llonga, for anyone thinking of visiting the island. Another great restaurant too is "SOS," situated right on the beach front and has a lovely ambience. We never want to leave the place that feels like our second home and the fabulous warm weather.

Sky dive
UHB Charity
July 9ᵗʰ, 2022

I had always said it would be nice to say thank you to the transplant team in some way and the hospital has some great ideas for encouraging people to fund raise. The Covid restrictions had at last been lifted. On one of our previous visits to the QE, I had picked up a copy of the UHB (University Hospitals Birmingham), charity magazine. The magazine gives information about several fundraising events including a skydive, which is something I had thought I might like to do. It seemed like the perfect timing for me to sign up for this and I felt it would be a great way of showing our appreciation to the hospital.

We set up a Just Giving page in February 2022 and within 2 days, this had reached our target of £800.00. We were completely overwhelmed with the kindness and generosity of family and friends, who had all shared our journey.

I managed to complete the skydive on 9th July 2022, with the superb team at Hinton Airfield, who provide fantastic support and are brilliant at giving you the confidence you need.

Hinton is an old wartime airfield, built in 1940, by the RAF Bomber Command, during the second world war. It closed to military activity in 1945, but today is still used for light aircraft, gliders and of course a skydiving centre. I felt surprisingly calm, but I was worried that when it came to the jump, I might panic and not be able to do it. I kept thinking how strong Richard had been to get to where he is and what he had been through, this was nothing in comparison. These were the thoughts that kept me positive all the way through.

It was an emotional moment when I was back in Richard's arms for a hug after completing the skydive. The total raised was just over £2000, which is a great start, but I hope in the future to raise even more.

We had the event filmed and when we arrived back home after the skydive, Richard couldn't wait to see the recording of it. It was a great day and we were so lucky with the weather. I went into the garden, to enjoy the sunshine and looked up to the sky thinking, crikey, I was up there not too long ago. I waited for Richard's reaction to the filming and he was elated, saying it was brilliant, I could hear him shouting and clapping. He called for me to come and watch it with him. Once again I found myself overcome with emotion, not really believing it was me who had jumped out of a plane and I felt like I was watching someone else. It was another fantastic moment to share. There could never be enough thanks given to the transplant team, but at least it was a start.

Thank you so much to all our family, friends and neighbours who so very kindly donated to the QE transplant team and who together have given the most incredible continued support to myself and Richard.

Hinton Airfield for the UHB charity

The link for University Hospitals Birmingham charity is **www.hospitalcharity.org** if anyone wishes to get involved or support and raise funds for the new **Edmonds Transplant Centre** due to be opened at the end of 2024. This will become a national centre of excellence for organ transplantation in Birmingham. The new centre will bring all the specialist care to patients, including pre-transplant consultations, additional fitness classes before surgery, patient support groups and rehabilitation classes after surgery.

Summary

Initially I wrote this book, in the hope it would be helpful and informative, to anyone who may find themselves in the same situation we faced, all those years ago. It isn't meant to alarm or frighten anyone, but is a true, honest account of what someone may experience, either with the prospect of having an LVAD, or a heart transplant. During the process of writing, it became something more, by telling our whole story and how love and endurance has brought us through.

Throughout our long journey there have been so many ups and downs, particularly during the Covid pandemic. It has been the longest and probably most difficult few years for us since the start of Richards health problems in 2011. In the beginning, we had to learn how to adjust and live with an unknown set of circumstances, from the fitting of the LVAD, then again since his transplant.

We are grateful every day and have promised that we will never become complacent about the gift of life that Richard has been given and how incredibly fortunate we are.

At the time, we believe Richard was the longest LVAD patient to be transplanted at the QE and to survive the procedure. That's quite a statistic for him to have on his medical record.

What a brilliant way to end this story and to say such a HUGE thank you to all involved with Richard's care, but ESPECIALLY to the organ donor family, who have selflessly given Richard the gift of life. Our future is looking much brighter because of them. One thing we know, is that rain or shine we will always be there for each other, in sickness and in health, till death do us part.

"Okay Richard, "It's time for some more Barry White."

Acknowledgements

It's impossible to mention all the staff, who were involved in looking after Richard during his long road to recovery, both at the Queen Elizabeth Hospital Birmingham and the Royal Stoke University Hospital. Not forgetting the first responders and paramedics, who transferred Richard to hospital so swiftly back in 2011, after his heart attack.

The skilled surgeons, alongside the theatre staff who got him through every step of the way, in what we know was the most difficult of operations. The ICU area C staff or Critical Care as its also known, who I never got the chance to meet due to Covid, but who cared for Richard around the clock. The Coronary Care unit and members of staff who I know pushed for my visits to happen when he moved wards. The brilliant staff on Ward 727 and Ward 304, including the ward managers who received this handover and made my visits a reality. The fantastic patient experience team, a vital service during Covid when communications with a loved one was so difficult.

The amazing transplant team and all the services involved for Richard's routine appointments and hospital stays. They have continued to care for Richard since 2012, never failing to achieve the best outcome they could for him. It goes without saying that they have all played an incredible part in his journey. They know who they are, should they read this story. I hope they acknowledge how much they mean to us both and the huge appreciation we have for them all.

I have to mention my brother David, who I spoke to nearly every day on the phone and who always manages to make me laugh, no matter what is happening. My close friends and work colleagues, who were always ready to listen if I had been going through a difficult patch. For all the friends and relatives who prayed for Richard, I know there were many,--your prayers were answered.

To Matts mum, for letting me share her sensitive story, it cannot have been easy for her to describe that day again, but I hope it will help others. The LVAD and heart transplant friends who we have met along the way. Some we have lost, some are still waiting for a transplant, and some have been successfully transplanted like Richard.

Our beautiful children and grandchildren, who haven't been mentioned too much, or I would need to write another book. They all continue to give us laughter and most of all love.

Kris, Max, Jenny, Nik, Kelly, Katie.

Grandchildren

James, Eleanor, Kristian, Jenson, Poppy, Isabelle, Luca, Evie, Leo, Riccardo, baby Myles

not forgetting Mitsy the Chihuahua

A huge thank you to Robert Lyell. We met Robert on holiday in November 2022, over a drink in the bar. Robert has put in many hours helping me with the editing of this book. I discovered during our conversations, he had done some writing for Bentley Motors. The friends and neighbours, who I have kept asking to read random chapters of the book, in the hope they would give me much needed feedback.

Jill and Allen, another couple we met in Cala Llonga, on our first return to Ibiza after Richards transplant. They have continued to ask and encourage me to get this book finished. All lovely friendships made whilst travelling. Carol and Liz, my forever Ibiza friends since the 1970's, their friendship and support has never changed in all the years I have known them.

For all those people waiting for a transplant, don't ever give up hope. It seems to happen when you least expect it. Keep trusting that anything is possible, especially if we all keep believing in life and love.

Lastly to my hubby and best friend, Richard, for fighting the fight, never giving up and most of all helping me with writing and sharing his incredible story.

Printed in Great Britain
by Amazon

34053515R00119